MY JOURNEY WITH GOD

TRAVELLING IN THE
SUPERNATURAL REALM

RHODA COLLINS
WORKING WITH ANGELS

Scripture references, unless otherwise noted, are in the Amplified Bible, Classic Edition

ISBN (Paperback): 978-0-9997429-8-3
ISBN (eBook): 978-0-9997429-9-0

WayOfTheEagle.org

Contents

DEDICATION

TO GOD THE FATHER AND YESHUA

"Blessed be the Lord, the God of Israel, from everlasting and to everlasting [from this age to the next, and forever]! Amen and Amen (so be it)."Psalm 41:13

"[For my concern is] that their hearts may be braced (comforted, cheered, and encouraged) as they are knit together in love, that they may come to have all the abounding wealth and blessings of assured conviction of understanding, and that they may become progressively more intimately acquainted with and may know more definitely and accurately and thoroughly that mystic secret of God, [which is] Christ (the Anointed One)." Colossians 2:2

TO MY BELOVED HUSBAND

A constant love and encouragement who taught me about operating in the spiritual realm.

TO MICHAEL TYRREL

Who created Wholetones, truly inspirational, frequency music, which assisted me with my journey with God.

INTRODUCTION

"Can a man be translated by faith?" Bruce Allen wrote in his book, "Translation by Faith."

In the book, "The Way-Visit Heaven Whenever You Want," written by my husband, Al Collins, God said:

"Father speaks to you now, "My rare ones, do not think that you are not of much importance. I call out to the hearts of every person to come to Me. Rest with Me. Allow Me to calm the storms that come against you. Allow Me to clear the paths and quench your thirst. What you search for is here. It rests with Me and in this Kingdom. The world cannot touch your heart but with a dead finger. My hand contains life everlasting. Reach out for it, and it is here. I will not refuse you nor reject you. I will soothe your wounds. Come to Heaven and accept your inheritance. It waits for you. Your crowns are here. Your treasures are here. Do not abandon them, as your portion is set before you for a reason. Your inheritance is offered to you now, to partake of as you walk in the world. Heaven is a place offered to all. My desires are that all could come to Me, to share their lives with Me, as I have a place for each in the Kingdom of Heaven. This Kingdom shall stand for eternity. The Kingdom is alive and a part of eternity, which is also alive. Each and everyone and everything have been designed for a purpose. You, My son and Rhoda and all who I have created are from my heart, from My love.

Every flower, every butterfly, every drop of water has a purpose. Each person is a precious, rare flower to me; a design that is of Me; a reflection of Me; a part of Me."

All of us can reach our full potential with Jesus Christ and Our Heavenly Father to fulfill our destiny. Nothing is impossible for those who believe and step out in faith to be translated by faith. The experiences that I am about to share with you were done with the Holy Spirit and are not fabricated. When you develop your relationship with Jesus in spirit and you step into Him daily and drink from His living water, your spirit expands to where your life becomes limitless.

"For with God nothing is ever impossible and no word from God shall be without power or impossible of fulfillment." Luke 1:37

"Delight yourself also in the Lord, and He will give you the desires and secret petitions of your heart." Psalm 37:4

"But without faith it is impossible to please and be satisfactory to Him. For whoever would come near to God must [necessarily] believe that God exists and that He is the rewarder of those who earnestly and diligently seek Him [out]." Hebrews 11:6

CHAPTER 1
MY JOURNEY WITH GOD BEGINS

My journey with God began in a deeper way, when I moved from California to Hungary in 1998. I was in bondage with self-gratification living by: I want, I think, I feel, even though I was a born-again Christian, I had no victory in my life as I was controlled by my flesh.

I was born in a communist country, behind the Iron Curtain, where Christians had limited freedom to worship God, except in the Orthodox religion, which was accepted by the communist government. People were allowed to attend certain churches, but in some villages, people were arrested and persecuted for their faith. For example, Baptists were not allowed to go to college because they were considered a cult. I grew up not knowing God, in a family where God was unknown. Once in a while my brother asked our mom, "Can you tell me more about God?" My mom would simply answer, "I don't know." My mother had a harsh life as a child growing up with parents who abused her mentally and emotionally. There were many seeds of rejection and curses planted in her blood line especially the ones that came down through her mother's ancestors. These are known as generational curses, that need to be broken on both sides of the family all the way back to Adam, which I had to do to release myself from demonic torment that afflicted me (discussed more later).

Exodus 34:6-7 says this about generational curses:

"And the Lord passed by before him, and proclaimed, The Lord! The Lord! A God merciful and gracious, slow to anger, and abundant in loving-kindness and truth, Keeping mercy and loving-kindness for thousands, forgiving iniquity and transgression and sin, but Who will by no means clear the guilty, visiting the iniquity of the fathers upon the children and the children's children, to the third and fourth generation."

Back to my parent's story - they were both hard, working-class citizens and both strong-willed. My father provided for the family, but he had a bad temper and he was very abusive verbally and physically towards my mom and me and sometimes towards my brother. My parents divorced years later, but the pain of such dramatic abuse left many scars in both of us. Later on, my mother abused me emotionally and verbally also, adding more wounds to my soul. I constantly had to forgive her.

How many of you know that your mama can be your trauma?

I grew up in a very unstable, volatile home environment and never really felt safe and secure throughout my childhood. Learning to trust God and walk with Him taught me to feel safe and secure in my life.

I was imagining and contemplating for a long time, how to escape this "place" that I considered a prison. I had this motto in my mind, "I am going to leave this place, move to the USA and live the life I always wanted."

I became a born-again Christian when I was 18, by listening to radio free Europe. It was the first time I heard a teaching, about being born-again. My brother tuned into the radio station and two days per week, we studied the Bible with the radio. We didn't have an actual Bible because you couldn't just buy one in a store; there was no such thing. Later my brother received a Bible from my father, which he borrowed from someone at work. We really enjoyed listening and studying the Bible through Radio Free Europe. After two years my brother said, "Let's find a church and go to worship God." But we didn't know which one to pick, so my brother decided that we should go to an Orthodox church. At first, I didn't agree with this decision, but I went with him anyway.

While there, I learned all the religious stuff that people do: recite lots of prayers from a religious book; confess to the priest; revere idols, etc., because I didn't know any better. At the end of two years I got so sick and tired of their dead, religious nonsense that I left. My brother never left. He's a fanatic, Orthodox to this day. He doesn't follow Jesus, Who is The only Way, The Truth and The Life.

One day, in 1987, I met a group of American students in a subway. I found out that they were born-again Christians working for Campus Crusade for Christ. They invited me to study the Bible with them at their student house. After two years of being discipled in the gospels with them, I went to a Baptist church to be baptized. I went there hoping to get baptized right away, but they told me that I needed to take a course first. After the course I finally got water baptized in 1990. Several months later in April the revolution came and all of Eastern Europe began moving away from communist suppression.

After five years of fellowship at a Baptist church an acquaintance invited me to a Pentecostal home group where I received the baptism of the Holy Spirit. It was an amazing experience! I felt a huge wave of the Spirit coming upon me and I started to pray in tongues. I was so excited about the Holy Spirit that I was praying in tongues all day long.

When I was 26 years old, I packed my bags and moved to California. When I got there, I thought, this is the "Promised Land." This place was like paradise to me in comparison to where I lived.

I was earnestly praying that God would allow me to stay in California.

Spiritually speaking, it was similar to the Jewish people living in bondage in Egypt. After two years of struggling, dealing with racism and dishonest people, that called themselves Christian, going nowhere, God took me out and planted me in Hungary. This wasn't the direction I planned for my life.

"A man's mind plans his way, but the Lord directs his steps and makes them sure." Proverbs 16:9

Just like Joseph was betrayed, and suffered persecution, that's how my life reflected to me at that time.

CHAPTER 2
MY WILDERNESS IN HUNGARY

Hungary became "wilderness" for me spiritually speaking. It was a place where God started a deep work in me, restoring and healing my life. When I moved to Hungary I thought "it was the end of the world" for me. I kept saying, "Lord, how could you do this to me? Surely this is not your will for me to stay here." There was so much pain and junk in my soul, I didn't know that I needed brokenness and a cleansing of my soul completely. Though my spirit was made perfect when I gave my life to Christ, my soul was heavy with pain. It was very wounded and desperately needed healing. The Lord gave me a promise in the midst of my agony.

He said, "I am going to take you back and bless you with a husband also."

This is what the Lord promised me on March 19, 2001:

"Trust Me and be patient My precious one. I love you and I have great plans for you. Pray and believe with all of your heart, I am with you and I know what is going to happen in your future. Something good is going to happen to you this year. Get ready for a haul of blessings. This is just the beginning. I am giving you this promise and I am asking you to believe it. Step by step I am taking you from glory to glory. I AM THE GOD OF YOUR LIFE. I will do much more for you. Ask and it shall be given to you. Even if you don't see something happen, trust Me, I know what's good for you. I know what's best for you. I love so much the mate that I am preparing for you. Get ready to meet him. He is precious, his heart is pure, and he is strong in Me. He is an Eagle Christian. He will fall in love with you from the first day he will see you. Don't underestimate yourself. Because of my Son I do this for you. Don't be afraid. I love My Son and I love you too. I am going to give you the best. No matter what happens, trust Me. I am with you. I care about your desires. I know what's in you. Trust me and depend on Me, relax in Me. When my timing comes, everything I said will happen."

Wow! This prophecy gave me so much hope and more trust in my Lord. He is worthy of all glory!

"Lean on, trust in, and be confident in the Lord with all your heart and mind and do not rely on your own insight or understanding. In all your ways know, recognize, and acknowledge Him, and He will direct and make straight and plain your paths." Proverbs 3:5-6

Father was teaching me to wait like an eagle on a rock, waiting for the unforced rhythms of grace, learning not to stay carnal, but to go beyond the flesh into a level of holiness and learning, to soar like an eagle above the storms. The eagle studies the storm and sits calmly on the rock and when he is ready to fly, he locks his eight-foot wing span and lets the currents of the wind lift him up and he begins to soar high up in the sky. I have learned patience and steadfast endurance while waiting on God. Jesus taught us by example to remain stable in every situation. Father was developing His character in me by using circumstances and people to shape me.

Hebrews 10:36 became my daily bread: *"For you have need of steadfast patience and endurance, so that you may perform and fully accomplish the will of God, and thus receive and carry away [and enjoy to the full] what is promised."*

On December 24, 1998, Jesus asked me to marry Him, as at that time I was just dating Him. This is what the Lord spoke to me, that I wrote in my journal:

"I want you to consider Me number one in your life in all areas, in your thoughts, in your mind, in your visions, in your dreams, in your body, in your eyes what you see, what you hear, what you touch, smell, in your hopes, in everything you do.

Everything that you breathe is Me. Let Me rule over your hopes, dreams and desires. Let Me be the ruler of your life; let Me guide you with the wonderful Holy Spirit. Your heart belongs totally to Me. I formed you in your mother's womb. I have placed this heart inside of you. I am guarding your heart with angels. I am guarding your heart with my anointed Word. Hold on to My promises, they are true, they are pure, I am going to give you the desires of your heart. But don't make this desire like an escape and an obsession. I am the One who rules over your dreams and desires. Trust in Me, hold on to Me. I am in control. Nothing will stand in your way because I have put My finger over your life. I love you with an infinite unending LOVE. Believe Me.

All is true what I have promised you. Just like I gave Abraham a son and when the promise came true, I asked him to sacrifice his son on the altar. So, I am asking you the same thing, sacrifice your desires on My Holy Altar. Don't be afraid. Let Me take care of your past. The battle belongs to Me. I Am sending angels to surround you.

You are my beloved child. I have a glorious future for you. I am strengthening you in this hour. Let me guide you in all freedom and truth. I Am the potter; you are the clay. I am making you into something beautiful that represents Me and brings Me glory. I Am your Heavenly Father; let me guide your emotions and your feelings. Pour your feelings into My

17

cup. Let Me form you and transform you. I am the God of your life Who knows about the future. If you walk on my path I am going to do so much in your life, I am going to bless you so much that almost you couldn't bear all the blessings I have for you. Trust Me, this transition period will not be without an end.

Soon I will move in your life, let Me guide you and prosper you. As you learn to wait upon Me, learn to be humble and obedient. I love you very much. My Son died for you. Recognize that His blood purifies you. He resurrected you and lives inside of your heart. Fix your eyes upon me. I am carrying you as a little lamb in My arms. Be pure and Holy in everything. I LOVE YOU."

This is very similar to what is written in *Deuteronomy 8: 2-8, "And you shall [earnestly] remember all the way which the Lord your God led you these forty years in the wilderness, to humble you and to prove you, to know what was in your [mind and] heart, whether you would keep His commandments or not. And He humbled you and allowed you to hunger and fed you with manna, which you did not know nor did your fathers know, that He might make you recognize and personally know that man does not live by bread only, but men lives by every word that proceeds out of the mouth of the Lord. Your clothing did not become old upon you nor did your feet swell these forty years. Know also in your [minds and] hearts that, as a man disciplines and instructs his son, so the Lord your God disciplines and instructs you. So, you shall keep the commandments of the Lord your God, to walk in His ways and [reverently] fear Him. For the Lord your God is bringing you into a good land, a land of brooks of water, of fountains and springs, flowing forth in valleys and hills; land of wheat and barley, and vines and fig trees and pomegranates, a land of olive trees and honey."*

I was fed with "manna" spiritually, studying Joyce Meyer's teaching tapes and being rooted and grounded in God's Word. One teaching tape was called, "This is Killing Me," which was fitting my situation perfectly. I went through years of being "killed in the flesh," learning to be led by the Spirit.God was refining me just like the scripture says, *"The refining pot is for silver and the furnace for gold, but the Lord tries the hearts." Proverbs 17:3*

These scriptures became more prominent in my life:

"But who can endure the day of His coming? And who can stand when He appears? For He is like a refiner's fire and like fullers' soap; He will sit as a refiner and purifier of silver, and He will purify the priests, the sons of Levi, and refine them like gold and silver, that they may offer to the Lord offerings in righteousness." Malachi 3:2-3

"Behold, I have refined you, but not as silver; I have tried and chosen you in the furnace of affliction." Isaiah 48:10

Those things that God wanted to change in my life started to burn and change me into pure gold with no dross. I was on the altar being "burned" and I was learning to go through the fire of transformation in order to enter the glory of God.

Father was also developing holiness in me just like the scripture in *Isaiah 35:8* says: *"A highway will be there a roadway, and it will be called a Highway of Holiness. The Highway of holiness is built in our hearts so Heaven can flow through us to the world around us."*

I was learning to present my body as a living sacrifice to become pure in heart.

In 1999 I received a prophecy from J. Clevenger who said: "You have a rainbow that represents a covenant between you and God. You will experience a full emotional and mental healing."

I didn't understand at that time, that in order to fully follow Christ meant to carry His cross. I practiced this through experience in my daily walk with the Lord in the wilderness. I have learned to praise God in hard times, and allow my Father to develop the character of an Eagle Christian. Too many Christians want the blessings in their lives, but without crucifixion of the flesh so that God's character would be developed in them. Many people want microwave-maturity. This is a myth in Christian circles.

I received another prophecy in 1999 from C. Madden: "God is preparing you for a mate and He is going to love you as much as Jesus loves you."

Wow, this confirmed what Father spoke to me earlier, and encouraged me, as it was my heart's desire to marry an Eagle Christian. As I was journaling all my experiences with God, I realized the depth of what God was doing in me. He was using people and circumstances to change me.

I was going through many storms at that time, but I learned, just like the eagle, to embrace the storm and soar above it to see the miracles of God unfolding in my life.

One particular storm was when I went to the International Church of Budapest, where, over the two years that I was there, I encountered several leaders that had baggage and their own personal agendas.

I loved the church because it was English speaking, with a mixture of people from so many different countries. I joined a home group led by a leader from Ellel Ministry in Hungary, who, for a time, was a mentor. Her and her husband had moved from California to East Europe and traveled often to England, which was the headquarters for Ellel ministry. I attended their seminars and learned about words of knowledge, prophecy and about false church teachings, like Easter was a pagan holiday, which surprised me. I eventually became part of the prayer team ministry.

God used this season to set me free from a past traumatic memory. I became trapped in a soul prison when I was 10 years old from experiencing a traumatic event watching my mother give birth to a child in the bathroom, who died on the floor. Jesus delivered me from that trauma that plagued me and I was set free. Praise God!

My relationship with this mentor was difficult, as she was a racist, demeaning and very manipulative and controlling (Christian witchcraft). I found out later she was sexually abused by her father for many years but was not completely healed on a mental, emotional or spiritual level. The Lord revealed to me that my relationship with this woman was phony, and, that she was planting seeds of rejection in my soul. Her true "colors" hit me like a tidal wave.

I left the church immediately, although the harm had already been done, as healing from this mentor and place took about two years.

The healing process from God involved Joyce Meyer's tapes, teaching me to pray for my enemies. I learned to pass several tests: the trusting test, the forgiveness test, the rejection test and the insecurity test. As soon as I decided to forgive and pray for that leader and others there, it shifted my focus to Jesus, gradually healing my emotions and my wounds.

I learned to walk it out and not allow my feelings to rule me. I decided to forgive and let go of past hurts.

Not rehearsing past hurts helped me to resist the temptation to think about how people hurt me in the past. I was learning to win the battlefield of the mind.I understood more practically what *Matthew* says in chapter *5:44-45: "But I tell you, Love your enemies and pray for those who persecute you, To show that you are the children of your Father Who is in Heaven; for He makes His sun rise on the wicked and on the good, and makes the rain fall upon the upright and the wrongdoers (alike)."*

My path was getting narrower and narrower and if I wanted to do great things for God, I had to pay the price to let Him do what He needed to be done in me and through me.

So, after I left this church, I found out from other sources, that she and her husband were "wolves in sheep's clothing." They'd been doing destructive things in other churches, leaving a trail of rejection everywhere they went and as a result many churches died. There was a huge spirit of rejection in the International Church in Budapest. Besides myself, many Christians were hurt by this woman and left, including the pastor. This woman was practicing Christian witchcraft over this pastor. He was so depressed that he said, "I have nothing left to give." She was misusing the power of God to manipulate him with her thoughts to remove him from his position.

Christian Witches are an abomination before the Lord

What is Christian witchcraft, that is rarely, if ever, talked about?

Well, the majority of Christians around the world are enslaved right now under what you can call Christian witches, although they aren't Christian.Shocking statement, but as you will see, easy enough to verify.

It's quite common for religious structures, churches, home groups and ministries worldwide to practice Christian witchcraft, either deliberately or in ignorance. Such as, children of God are easily deceived when they have leaders who charm them, deceive them or guilt them to stay under their covering which is a religious, man-made hierarchy and not what God the Father intended for your life. We are to be searching God's will for our life, not some religious leader's.

People are deceived by Christian witches in some of the following ways:

1. Control through fear and intimidation
2. Anger and frustration to influence other's mood, attitude and decisions
3. Utilizing false doctrines/heresy and anti/contra/cherry picked-Gospel teachings to achieve results
4. They pray (sorcery) for people's will to follow their own will/ personal agendas
5. They bind (sorcery) people's will to force and manipulate them in the spirit

All of this activity is demonic, activating evil spirits to assist these witches in their work. Christian witches are any who pretend to use the Word of God and His power with the aim of influencing people to achieve their own selfish purposes.

"Now the practices of the sinful nature are clearly evident: they are sexual immorality, impurity, sensuality (total irresponsibility, lack of self-control), idolatry, sorcery, hostility, strife, jealousy, fits of anger, disputes, dissensions, factions [that promote heresies]." Galatians 5:19-20

Christian witches use works of the flesh and false prophesies to influence and control others.

"For you endure it if a man assumes control of your souls and makes slaves of you, or devours [your substance, spends your money] and preys upon you, or deceives and takes advantage of you, or is arrogant and puts on airs, or strikes you in the face." 2 Corinthians 11:20

They can also manipulate through hatred, strife and lust. Powers of lust, sexual desires and evil thoughts and imagination can manipulate and seduce a person.

"Strip yourselves of your former nature [put off and discard your old unrenewed self] which characterized your previous manner of life and becomes corrupt through lusts and desires that spring from delusion; And be constantly renewed in the spirit of your mind [having a fresh mental and spiritual attitude], And put on the new nature (the regenerate self) created in God's image, [Godlike] in true righteousness and holiness." Ephesians 4:22-24

Prayer made by Christian witches are selfish, soulish prayers endeavouring to put pressure on the mind, will and emotions of another with the aim of achieving their own desires. For example, praying for a marriage breakup so they can marry one of the former spouses. Or, praying that people give them more money.

A Christian witchcraft prayer engages or authorizes evil spirits to organize circumstances in such a manner to have that evil prayer answered. When someone allows their own desires and will to rule over the will of God or another person's will, they open themselves up to a spirit of deception that will take control of their will and emotions.
They are totally deceived and unaware that their prayers have become charismatic witchcraft.

It's very dangerous to pray into a situation without finding out God's will first.

People manipulate others through word curses, gossiping and backstabbing, which are all also witchcraft and rebellion.

Many people consult so-called prophets in the hope of receiving a Word from God. People who continually seek out a prophetic word can actually fall into fortune telling and divination and come under the influence of evil spirits.

"They have seen falsehood and lying divination, saying, The Lord says; but the Lord has not sent them. Yet they have hoped and made men to hope for the confirmation of their word." Ezekiel 13:6

There are also leaders/people who have what's called a Jezebel spirit, that manifest in some of the following ways:

1. Manipulates by weaponizing guilt and fear (trick people into doing things their way).
2. Dominates-Fight for control (make people do things their way)
3. Intimidate-Fear and rules (scare people in doing things their way).

Demonic power against you can feel like spiritual daggers or heaviness in your mind and heart, leaving you tired, frustrated, feeling oppressed, depressed, defeated, suicidal and no boldness to pray.

Deal with it.

Get rid of all such people from your life, if you want to move forward with God and your true eternal destiny.

Christian Racism

In addition to what I experienced at the International Church of Budapest, throughout my journey with God, I have encountered many racist Christians with a superior, elitist, entitled attitude, that caused them to mistreat me. Racism is a burning issue all over the world but especially in Western culture. One may define racism as the conviction that not all humans are equal, but that some are 'worthier' than others. Usually those who are regarded as 'unworthy humans' are not treated on par with the rest.

It's argued that the roots of racism in the Western world date back to the 1st century CE when the early Christians severed their ties with the Jewish people and their religion, and started humiliating and denigrating them. Traces of this can be found in the New Testament in *John 8:44, Revelation 2:9* and *3:9.*

"You are of your father, the devil, and it is your will to practice the lusts and gratify the desires [which are characteristic] of your father. He was a murderer from the beginning and does not stand in the truth, because there is no truth in him. When he speaks a falsehood, he speaks what is natural to him, for he is a liar [himself] and the father of lies and of all that is false." John 8:44

Christians considered the Jewish people and their synagogues to be associated with the devil. The apostle Paul contributed to the anti-Judaism sentiments of early Christians when he argued that the gospel superseded the law.This eventually led to the conviction that Christianity superseded Judaism, and that Jews and Judaism ranked lower than Christians and Christianity. These beliefs created fertile soil for the development of racism in the Western world. In the history of Christianity, the Roman Empire became the state religion and the dominant religion in the Western world, and the religious convictions fed into the sociopolitical and economic policies of the Western world.

This cancer grew into a mixture of racism, prejudice and discrimination against not only people of different ethnic backgrounds but also against Christians from different denominations, groups or viewpoints.

A personal example of this hybrid racism is when I encountered "Christians" in the U.S.A, especially in California. When they heard where I was born and about my spiritual outlook on God's Word, they called me a communist or some other nasty name to my face (I can only imagine what was said behind my back). They preened around like peacocks with their high-minded attitudes that they were better Christians than anyone else.

I've encountered racism by "Christians" in virtually every church, group or individual I've come in contact with. Catholics think they're better than Protestants, all of who Pentecostals say aren't as good as them, all of which are afflicted with pride and Christian racism within their various denominations. My own brother tells me I'm in a cult, because I operate my life with the Holy Spirit and won't bend to an Orthodox priest's will like he and his family do. It's all idiotic, chaotic and demonic.

Rarely have I found equal footing, with those who are suppose to be my brethren under God.

This is likewise Christian witchcraft.

I also encountered racism from non-Christians in the colleges and workplaces in Canada and as a result I was ostracized and persecuted not only for being a Christian but also because I was a foreigner.

The devil used these people to attack my identity over and over again and also in an effort to steal my Crown of Authority. But they couldn't succeed because I know who I am in Christ. My identity is not defined by a culture, the car I drive, the money I have, my status nor a spot on the planet where my mom gave birth to me. I rule from my mountain. I am seated at the right hand of my Father and I am a royal-priest and I am complete in Him Who is the head of all principalities and powers *(Colossians 2:10).*

You can quickly search God's Word for what leaders, Christians and fellowships should be doing, verses what you're experiencing. If they're doing something else, God says they're cursed.

"But even if we or an angel from Heaven should preach to you a gospel contrary to and different from that which we preached to you, let him be accursed (anathema, devoted to destruction, doomed to eternal punishment)! As we said before, so I now say again: If anyone is preaching to you a gospel different from or contrary to that which you received [from us], let him be accursed (anathema, devoted to destruction, doomed to eternal punishment)!" Galatians 1:8-9

If you choose to ignore God's warning because you prefer to live under false leaders, false doctrines, with false Christians, then this scripture applies to you too.

How to get Free?

In order to be free from manipulative religious structures/leaders, Christian racists, Christian witches, wrong friends/family etc., you can do the following:

1. Make a definite decision to live a Holy Spirit controlled life always acknowledging God in all of your ways, developing the fruit of the Spirit and crucify your flesh daily. You can do this by applying the Word of God, daily confessing and repenting of any sins. Search your own heart and motivations carefully and turn away and ask forgiveness of all witchcraft, manipulation and unlawful control you have exercised over others.

2. Break all soul ties that you've made with wrong people and associations.

3. Break all curses you've said against yourself, that others have said against you and that you've brought against yourself through sinful thoughts, words and deeds.

4. Break the generational sins and curses of manipulation and control coming down generations on both sides of your parents all the way back to Adam.

5. Stand fast on the promises of God that racism and witchcraft have no power over you when you are in Christ and Christ is in you.

6. Resist the power of the flesh by the power of the Holy Spirit.

7. Take communion every day. Applying the blood of Jesus can change your DNA and heal you completely.

You can pray the following prayer for yourself:

"Father, I exalt Your Name and praise You. There is nothing too difficult for You. I thank You that You can deliver me from anything evil including manipulation, fear, control, curses and witchcraft. I come against any curse and Christian witchcraft that's been applied or sent against me. I use the name of Jesus as a barrier to break those demonic powers and cast them away, commanding them to go to a spiritual prison, never to return. I use the blood of Jesus like a mighty wall to surround me and protect me from all demonic forces, curses and of witchcraft.

Prayer for another afflicted by evil powers, religion, racism, witchcraft, curses and the world:

Now I pray specifically for (_____) and ask You to destroy every soul power used against them, every spirit of witchcraft that deceived them, every carnal manipulation that would draw them into bondage of lust, strife, hatred or any other works of the flesh. I bind any and all evil spirits that work against them and break the bondages and strongholds that they have over that person in the Mighty Name of Jesus. I cast them out and command them to go to a spiritual prison and stay there until they are called to judgement by Jesus Christ.

I thank You Father, that while I see the walls of bondage fall, I will ask the Holy Spirit to convict my beloved of sin, righteousness and judgement. I ask You Holy Spirit to draw them to/back to Jesus so that they will apply Your righteousness.

I ask and plead the blood of Jesus over their minds to protect them against further demonic witchcraft powers. I pray that they will no longer be influenced or controlled by any person or thing.I thank You Lord for total deliverance and total healing for this person in the Mighty name of Jesus. Amen."

Back to my Journey with God…

After a period of time, the Lord led me to Danube International Church in Budapest. There were about a hundred people attending there, but only five people were baptized in the Holy Spirit. I wanted to be in a place where I could unwind, heal and be away from backstabbers, to just be accepted and not harassed, so I stayed. I developed good relationships with women and started attending a Bible study group.

I met Linda a very sweet lady, who also became my tutor to further develop myself in the English language, as I was preparing to pass the TOEFL test for International College. She was so kind-hearted and loved the Lord. God was using this opportunity to prepare me to go to college overseas. I prayed for two years to hear from God on what college He wanted me to attend. Finally, Jesus led me to go to Niagara College in Canada.

I said, "Canada?" I'd never thought of that.

There was still so much commotion in my life at that moment but now I was really excited to leave the wilderness life in Hungary to head out on my journey adventure with God into the unknown.

Chapter 2

CHAPTER 3
TO THE EDGE OF THE PROMISED LAND

In 2006 I was accepted at Niagara College, got my visa and moved to Canada.After I graduated two years later, I got a job working in the kitchen of a restaurant in Niagara Falls, which was physically demanding work, dealing with more challenging people and was living in a run-down apartment building in downtown Niagara Falls. Not exactly what I pictured the Promised Land to look like.

After two years of this life, I cried out to God, "Just please give me someone in my life that would love me and not harass me." I was so tired of dealing with bullies. I didn't have to wait too long. A week after my plea to God, I walked by a small place about a block from where I lived, that had eagle statues displayed in their window. It was a street ministry that was heavily involved in spiritual warfare.

I walked inside and was met by the hosts of this Christian gathering. While we were talking about the eagles in their window that attracted me, I told them that I'd received a prophecy that I will marry a strong man of God who was a true Eagle Christian. I asked if they knew of such a person.

The one host thought for a while and said, "Al's an Eagle."

I said, "Who's Al?"

She said, "You need to meet him."

I was amazed to hear this good news and also eager to meet this mysterious Eagleman that may be the one that God had for me.

The next day I went to this fellowship and met Al's cousin who lived across the border in the U.S.A. Al hadn't been to this gathering in several weeks, as I'd been told, he was tending to his dying mother.

Several days later there was a street festival in downtown Niagara Falls. Al's cousin walked up to me with this white-bearded man and said, "This is Al."

I looked straight into his eyes and thought, "Eagle's eyes, wow!" His eyes were piercing, sharp and intense.

We talked quite a bit and one day Al offered to take me to a place in Niagara-on-the-Lake I hadn't seen. While Al was driving, I told him that God is preparing me to marry an Eagle Christian, who's an American and a Canadian. When he heard that he was very surprised. He said, "You're supposed to marry an American who's a Canadian and an Eagle Christian?"

"Yes," I replied.

He said, "Not very many around." (Al has Canadian and American citizenship).

When he went home, he asked God, "What's going on here?"

Father said to him, "This is the purple flower I have prepared for you for many years."

Al said, "She's too young for me."

Father said, "Don't worry about it."

Al said, "She's from Hungary. What are we going to talk about?"

Father said, "Don't worry about it."

Al asked, "I'm older than her. What's going to happen after I'm gone?"

Father said, "Do you trust me?"

Al said, "Yes."

Father said, "So, don't worry about it."

While Al was doing that, I still didn't realize that God the Father had chosen Al to be my husband. I went home and said to the Lord, "He's a nice man, but he's too old for me Lord," as I wanted to marry someone younger.

Next Sunday we met again and both of us were on fire for God and talking about Him all the time. Al told me about the whole conversation he had with Father, about me being his choice and the purple flower He chose for me and I was amazed and surprised at the same time.

So a week later, during the worship in the church, I heard Father saying to me just like vows when someone marries somebody, "I, Rhoda, take thee, Al, to be my wedded husband, to have and to hold, from this day forward, for better, for worse, for richer, for poorer, in sickness and in health, to love and to cherish, till death do us part, according to God's holy ordinance; and thereto I pledge thee my faith, pledge myself to you." I understood that Al was God's choice for me to marry. Father God is very creative in His promises.

Al and I were sitting on a couch one day after this and he had his arm on my shoulder. He felt an electric fire going back and forth from my body to his. Al asked Father, "What is this?"

He said, "I am joining you in the Spirit."

Al asked God, "Is that biblical?

Father said, *"What God has joined together let man not put asunder." (Matthew 19:6)*

A few days later the Lord took me in the spirit and I saw the following:

"In the summer of 2008, I saw Al and I walking up stairs in Heaven. We were both wearing white robes. We met Jesus at the top of the stairs. Jesus was wearing a bright, white robe with a hood. We both knelt in front of Jesus as He put a Jewish tallit on our heads and on top of that He put an opened Bible with a shining, bright sword on top of the Bible. Then He bent down and put rings on both of our fingers. Jesus married us in the Spirit. Praise God. Hallelujah!"

This is what Al wrote in his journal after he met me:

"I was impressed with Rhoda's uncompromising dedication to God. She has a fierce obedience and dedication to God- to do His will. She is a true Eagle Christian with a constant thirst and hunger for more of God and developing herself spiritually. I realized that she was a rare warrior-conqueror in God's kingdom. I enjoyed many of our talks on spiritual things and thought that she will be a huge threat to the evil kingdom. I really didn't consider her as someone to date, as I was waiting for God to choose my wife.

When she told me God's prophecies concerning her future husband it seemed to point to me. So, I went to God in prayer and He told me, "She is the purple flower that I have chosen for you; cherish this gift." My concerns were overcome when God the Father pointed out to me that I had total faith and trust in Him. "Thank You Father for the lovely flower named Rhoda that you have brought to me for us to be together. We live for You, Father. Amen."

During this time, the devil was not idle. We both were attending the street-ministry where I had found out about Al. At this time, we also visited many other fellowships, which angered the leader of the street-ministry, who also happened to be a close friend of Al's for twenty years. This leader yelled at us for going somewhere else, which surprised Al, as this leader had never acted this way towards him before. The atmosphere in the church changed as soon as Al and I started dating. The devil was at work trying to keep us apart through anyone around us, because together he knew that we'd do a lot of damage to his kingdom.

We found out one of the other leaders, was bad-mouthing us behind our back. And, there was a woman, also a leader, who was secretly very jealous of me that was spreading lies about me to the head leader's wife telling her that I was a witch, in an effort to lure Al away from me for herself. The wife, because of her immaturity in Christ, as she was a new Christian, believed this woman and so, she started to attack us verbally. She told Al that he was either blind or stupid not to see that I was a witch. People like that get easily deceived by familiar spirits as they don't have discernment.

While this was happening, I found out that they were knowingly allowing fornicators to lead and be on the worship team. I showed Al's "good friend" the scriptures in *1 Corinthians 5* that we shouldn't associate with anyone who calls themselves a Christian and lives like a swindler,

37

fornicator, drunkard, etc. We're actually supposed to hand them over to satan *(v.5)*. He waved me away saying that we weren't Corinthians. This "friend" joined the rest in attacking Al about our relationship. Even Al's cousin joined in on the Judas-fest. Christian witchcraft reared its head again.

I said to Al that I didn't want to associate with people who grieve the Holy Spirit. Al was fed up with them too. It's hard to walk away from some people, but you have to decide if you're going to be a God-pleaser or a people-pleaser.

Al and I left and sure enough, that small street ministry withered away. Once leaders become wolves and allow wolves in the camp, the Holy Spirit leaves and the sheep get devoured or scatter.

Al and I were married in November 2008 in Niagara Falls and spent our honeymoon on the beautiful island of Maui, Hawaii. God fulfilled my dreams, as Hawaii was part of it. Praise God! He's so faithful!

So, we began our journey together with God, developing our relationship with Him in the spiritual realm. I believe Jesus is calling me to wage war with the Holy Spirit in the spirit, but also to travel in the spiritual realm to many places to bring healing, raise the dead and set captives free.

Jesus asks me to write this book, My Journey with God

I went in the spirit and started dancing in twirls with Jesus. We were in this beautiful meadow surrounded by dogwood trees with pink flowers. We were having a party in the meadow, with angels playing the flute.

After that, I saw Father sitting at a table like a judge, calling out people's names to give them a scroll. It was like a graduation ceremony. Al and I received a scroll with a red ribbon.

Jesus said to me, "I want you to write a book: My Journey with God. Take everything from journals and newsletters and put them in a file, invest your time in this."

I told Him that I didn't know how to write and that He needed to help me with it.

Then this happened,

100 Scrolls

I went in the spirit to the Father's throne room and I cast my crown before Him. He put it back on my head and invited me to sit next to Him on my Seat of Authority. Jesus came, hugged me and said, "I assigned these angels to assist you with the book." (Meaning, to write this book). An angel brought a sack of scrolls (100 of them) and we took them to the library of Heaven and put them on a shelf. Jesus then told me to eat the scrolls. I ate all of them. On one scroll was written:

"It all began with a desire to get to know Jesus intimately to develop all my spiritual senses and travel in the spiritual realm with Him and do miracles. The desire grew to the point that I wanted more of Him, never get satisfied. He is everything to me. He leads me, guides me and loves me beyond measure. One of the scrolls (red color) that I ate tasted like honey. There was also a black scroll that I had to eat and hesitated but once Jesus covered it with His blood I decided to eat the scroll."

This book, that God asked me to write, was to teach others how to make their journey with God a reality and to share my wonderful journeys to offer hope, faith and encouragement for others to partake of their treasures in Heaven and with God now.

CHAPTER 4
VENTURING OUT
IN THE SUPERNATURAL REALM

We are living in multidimensional realms and as spirit-beings, we have the ability to travel in the past, present or future. Time is only limited to the physical dimensions.

I understand that it's difficult for people to understand or even believe that this is possible as they've been taught and experienced only life in the physical realm. Most refuse to believe even when countless testimonies pour in of people engaging with God in ways even beyond our imagination.

"But, on the contrary, as the Scripture says, What eye has not seen and ear has not heard and has not entered into the heart of man, [all that] God has prepared (made and keeps ready) for those who love Him [who hold Him in affectionate reverence, promptly obeying Him and gratefully recognizing the benefits He has bestowed]." 1 Corinthians 2:9

"Now to Him Who, by (in consequence of) the [action of His] power that is at work within us, is able to [carry out His purpose and] do superabundantly, far over and above all that we [dare] ask or think [infinitely beyond our highest prayers, desires, thoughts, hopes, or dreams]." Ephesians 3:20

There are many testimonies in the Bible from John, Phillip, Elijah and Ezekiel that all translated and transported in the spirit.

Jesus did many supernatural miracles and traveled in the supernatural realm.

For example, in *Matthew 8:13* Jesus healed the Roman centurion servant while physically far away: *"Then to the centurion Jesus said, go; it shall be done for you as you have believed. And the servant boy was restored to health at that very moment."*

God says that we are His children *(1 John 3)*, we are royal-priests *(1 Peter 2:9)*, we are more than conquerors *(Romans 8:37)*, we are saints *(Ephesians 2:19),* we are co-heirs with Christ *(Romans 8:17)*, we are seated with Christ right now in Heaven *(Ephesians 2:6)* and we have access to the Father right now *(Ephesians 2:8).*

The devil doesn't want you to know all that. He doesn't want you actively working against him. He doesn't want you to have a relationship with God. He doesn't want you to move forward with your destiny. He doesn't want you to have your inheritance. He wants people to stay spiritually handicapped in some fantasy world that will keep them entertained and out of the way until they die. Don't let him or anyone else steal your life.

If anyone is telling you anything different than what God says in His Word about who you are and what is available to you right now, then you need to make a decision.

You don't want Jesus saying this about you,

"I know your [record of] works and what you are doing; you are neither cold nor hot. Would that you were cold or hot!

So, because you are lukewarm and neither cold nor hot, I will spew you out of My mouth!

For you say, I am rich; I have prospered and grown wealthy, and I am in need of nothing; and you do not realize and understand that you are wretched, pitiable, poor, blind, and naked." Revelation 3:15-17

Getting Started

In the following chapters I'll be describing my continuing journey with Jesus, Father and angels along with further teaching to assist you in your journey. Much of it will be about my travels in the spirit into the supernatural realm doing high-level spiritual warfare and healing in the spirit.

Now before you get involved in spiritual warfare, please be sure that you're seated right with God.

"Hunting in the spirit is quantum leap years beyond big game hunting in the natural." The Silver Bullet of God - Al Collins

Spiritual warfare is a fantastic view of seeing and battling in the spiritual realm by partnership not only with Jesus Christ and God the Father and the Holy Spirit, but also together with the canopy of angels receiving and fulfilling scrolls from the strategy room in Heaven. There are many Courts in Heaven that you can also explore with Jesus.

I would not recommend that anyone do this kind of warfare if you don't have holiness in your life and/or if you live in sin or if you compromise with God's Word. Don't attack evil spirits if you live a sinful lifestyle, because they can literally destroy you.

Believe who you are in Christ

Our identity is very important in this process because many Christians don't know their authority and don't know who they are in Christ.

Below is a list that will reinforce your current identity in Christ. Go through it many times and let God's truth become your truth:

I am complete in Him Who is the Head of all principality and power *(Colossians 2:10).*

I am alive with Christ *(Ephesians 2:5).*

I am free from the law of sin and death *(Romans 8:2).*

I am far from oppression, and fear does not come near me *(Isaiah 54:14).*

I am born of God, and the evil one does not touch me *(1 John 5:18).*

I am holy and without blame before Him in love *(2 Peter 1:16; Ephesians 1:4).*

I have the mind of Christ *(Philippians 2:5; I Corinthians 2:16).*

I have the peace of God that passes all understanding *(Philippians 4:7).*

I have the Greater One living in me; greater is He Who is in me than he who is in the world *(1 John 4:4).*

I have received the gift of righteousness and reign as a king in life by Jesus Christ *(Romans 5:17)*.

I have received the spirit of wisdom and revelation in the knowledge of Jesus, the eyes of my understanding being enlightened *(Ephesians 1:17-18)*.

I have received the power of the Holy Spirit to lay hands on the sick and see them recover, to cast out demons, to speak with new tongues. I have power over all the power of the enemy, and nothing shall by any means harm me *(Mark 16:17-18; Luke 10:17,19)*.

I have put off the old man and have put on the new man, which is renewed in the knowledge after the image of Him Who created me *(Colossians 3:9,10)*.

I have given, and it is given to me; good measure, pressed down, shaken together, and running over, men give into my bosom *(Luke 6:38)*.

I have no lack for my God supplies all of my need according to His riches in glory by Christ Jesus *(Philippians 4:19)*.

I can quench all the fiery darts of the wicked one with my shield of faith *(Ephesians 6:16)*.

I can do all things through Christ Jesus *(Philippians 4:13)*.

I shall do even greater works than Christ Jesus *(John 14:12)*.

I show forth the praises of God Who has called me out of darkness into His marvelous light *(1 Peter 2:9)*.

I am God's child-for I am born-again of the incorruptible seed of the Word of God, which lives and abides forever *(1 Peter 1:23)*.

I am God's workmanship, created in Christ unto good works *(Ephesians 2:10)*.

I am a new creature in Christ *(2 Corinthians 5:17)*.

I am a spirit being-alive to God *(1 Thessalonians 5:23; Romans 6:11)*.

I am a believer, and the light of the Gospel shines in my mind *(2 Corinthians 4:4)*.

I am a doer of the Word and blessed in my actions *(James 1:22,25)*.

I am a joint-heir with Christ *(Romans 8:17)*.

I am more than a conqueror through Him Who loves me *(Romans 8:37)*.

I am an overcomer by the blood of the Lamb and the word of my testimony *(Revelation 12:11)*.

I am a partaker of His divine nature *(2 Peter 1:3,4)*.

I am an ambassador for Christ *(2 Corinthians 5:20)*.

I am part of a chosen generation, a royal priesthood, a holy nation, a purchased people *(1 Peter 2:9)*.

I am the righteousness of God in Jesus Christ *(2 Corinthians 5:21)*

I am the temple of the Holy Spirit; I am not my own *(1 Corinthians 6:19)*.

I am the head and not the tail; I am above and not beneath *(Deuteronomy 28:13)*.

I am the light of the world *(Matthew 5:14)*.

I am His elect, full of mercy, kindness, humility, and longsuffering *(Romans 8:33; Colossians 3:12)*.

I am forgiven of all my sins and washed in the Blood *(Ephesians 1:7)*.

I am delivered from the power of darkness and translated into God's kingdom *(Colossians 1:13)*.

I am redeemed from the curse of sin, sickness, and poverty *(Galatians 3:13; Deuteronomy 28:15-68)*.

I am firmly rooted, built up, established in my faith and overflowing with gratitude *(Colossians 2:7)*.

I am called of God to be the voice of His praise *(2 Timothy 1:9; Psalm 66:8)*.

I am healed by the stripes of Jesus *(1 Peter 2:24; Isaiah 53:5)*.

I am raised up with Christ and seated in Heavenly places *(Colossians 2:12; Ephesians 2:6)*.

I am greatly loved by God *(Colossians 3:12; Romans 1:7; 1 Thessalonians 1:4; Ephesians 2:4)*.

I am strengthened with all might according to His glorious power *(Colossians 1:11).*

I am submitted to God, and the devil flees from me because I resist him in the Name of Jesus *(James 4:7).*

I press on toward the goal to win the prize to which God in Christ Jesus is calling us upward *(Philippians 3:14).*

For God has not given us a spirit of fear; but of power, love, and a sound mind *(2 Timothy 1:7).*

It is not I who live, but Christ lives in me *(Galatians 2:20).*

All of the above states who you are now in Christ.

Reflecting Light or Darkness

Jesus said in *Matthew 5:14-16, "You are the light of [Christ to] the world. A city set on a hill cannot be hidden; nor does anyone light a lamp and put it under a basket, but on a lamp stand, and it gives light to all who are in the house. Let your light shine before men in such a way that they may see your good deeds and moral excellence, and [recognize and honor and] glorify your Father who is in Heaven."*

"Once more Jesus addressed the crowd. He said, "I am the Light of the world. He who follows Me will not walk in the darkness, but will have the Light of life." John 8:12

"For You cause my lamp to be lighted and to shine; The LORD my God illumines my darkness." Psalm 18:28

"But the path of the just (righteous) is like the light of dawn, that shines brighter and brighter until [it reaches its full strength and glory in] the perfect day." Proverbs 4:18

"The eye is the lamp of the body; so, if your eye is clear [spiritually perceptive], your whole body will be full of light [benefiting from God's precepts]." Matthew 6:22

These verses say that we are to be a light. Matthew says, that what we look at will reflect inside of us. Images and words have power, so it's very important that we screen very carefully what we watch on TV, on the internet, video games, what books and magazines we read, who we spend time with or what spiritually-dead "church" we attend, etc. If you watch a movie or play a game or read a book with violent or worldly content in it, part of that negativity and darkness will go inside of you. A spiritually-dead "church" can only provide flesh-driven activities to you, which, *"those who are in the flesh cannot please God" Romans 8:5-8.*

When someone isn't pleasing God, how can they operate in the supernatural?

How can they fulfill their destiny?

As you spend time with and soak in the presence of the Lord; read and engage with the Word of God; associate with spiritually-alive leaders and people; seek God first *(Matthew 6:33)* and seek to fill yourself with God's presence and Light, you will reflect Light which is Jesus, and darkness will be pushed out. Your spirit will move out of being dormant, to being active.

We were made in God's image to reflect Him. We have Jesus inside of us, as we, not some building, are His temple (1 Corinthians 3:16).

49

We are to reflect His Light.

See yourself as a Light receptor and soak up the Light of God.

If people don't know God on a personal level, then how can they be a reflection of Him?

How can they operate in spiritual realms?

You can't mirror someone whom you don't know. Your true identity lays in God the Father and His Son, Jesus and the Holy Spirit. We are sons and daughters of God. Christians need to think and act like royalty, that have position, power and authority who can move in Heavenly realms-now.

We also enter the Kingdom of God by faith, praise, worship, thanksgiving, working with the Holy Spirit, etc. Our spirit is awakened by many switches that we can operate. Not just once or here and there when we have time. We need to develop our spiritual muscles, just as we do our physical muscles, to get into shape. Practice developing your spiritual senses: hearing, seeing, touching, smelling and tasting. Spend time every day at it. We've discussed Christian witchcraft, Christian racism, curses, generational curses and wrong people that can hinder your Journey with God and your destiny, so let's look at some other areas how you can engage God in Heaven.

Your Gates

A person is made up of more than one body that has many gateways. These gateways can be blocked in many ways which can affect the way you are able to function properly and fully as a child of God.

It's very important during your personal time with Jesus to cleanse all of your body and soul gates. (There's a book that can help you with that called, "Gateways-The Three-Fold Nature of Man" by Ian Clayton).

Specifically, you need to let God develop your Christ-like character and sanctify your imagination gate by pleading the blood of Jesus over this gate for you to see in the spiritual realm. The same process is done with all the other gates: mind, will, emotions, conscience, reasoning, etc.

Engaging with God in Heaven

We engage God's DNA as light, sound frequency and vibration and we engage the four faces of God... YOD Hey Vav Hei.

The meaning of YHVH – Yod – Hei – Vav – Hei

YOD- LION- Spirit of the Lord and Fear of the Lord. Yod means palm the entire hand

HEI- OX- Spirit of Might. It means to show or reveal

VAV-EAGLE- Spirit of Wisdom and Knowledge. It signifies a nail, peg or a hook

HEI-MAN- Spirit of counsel and understanding

We physically carry the shapes of the Hebrew letters of His Holy Name.

The yod neatly fits your head.

Your arms fit the shape of the hei.

The elongated vav represents your spine.

And the final hei fits the shape of your legs.

There are nine strands of DNA that have multiple levels of revelation: character, nature, precepts and eternity.

Mike Parsons said:

"There are four dimensions in which we can engage with the Heavenly Father:

- Engage in the Earth, the physical realm, but in the spiritual realm of an open Heaven.
- Engage in our spirit and heart, the spiritual dimension. (Four Chambers of the Heart)
- Engage in the Heavenly realms – at the throne room, Garden of Eden, the mountain of God
- Engage God's heart in eternity, outside of time and space (creating your own galaxy).

When we engage the Heavenly Father in different dimensions, we create a window where infinity can manifest here and now to create what will be; so, the end and beginning will be in agreement and history will unfold in alignment with the Father's heart.

The Kingdom of Heaven is comprised in increasing levels of governmental authority relating to our maturity and positions:

1. Kingdom of God – Lordship
2. Kingdom of Heaven – Kingship
3. Heaven- Kingship and Sonship
4. Heaven of Heaven –Mature sons"

Angels

While moving around in the spiritual realm you will encounter angels. They wait for the children of God to wake up from their spiritual slumber in order to serve them.

"Are not the angels all ministering spirits (servants) sent out in the service [of God for the assistance] of those who are to inherit salvation?" Hebrews 1:14

At first, they may astonish you as they are quite amazing. Don't revere them. Work with them, as God will place them at your disposal to assist in accomplishing His will in your life.

There are many kinds of angels with different ranks that you will encounter, beyond guardian angels that most people have heard of:

1. Warrior Angels called Sandelphon
2. Cherubim –Covering ones- Raphael
3. Sons of God- Michael- Banai-Elohim
4. Judges- Elohim- Haniel
5. Messengers- Malachim- Uriel
6. Burning Ones- Seraphim- Gabriel
7. Shining Ones- Chashmalim –Tzadkiel
8. Mighty Ones- Erelim- Tzaphkiel
9. Spheres- Ofanim- Raziel
10.Creatures- Chayoth- Metraton

Evil angels, principalities, powers and demons

While in the spiritual realm, you will also encounter evil spirits of various kinds. Thinking you won't encounter them is foolish, as they are at war with you 24/7 so best not to stick your head in the sand, thinking that ignoring them will make them go away or as some under doctrines that says, "spiritual warfare is no longer needed, as we're beyond that old-fashioned age".

Satan is called the power and prince of the air *(Ephesians 2:2)*. He has many spiritual beings under his control and most of the population of the earth are his puppets. Good news is, they are contained in, on and around the earth.

The atmosphere of the earth is made up of three spheres: rules, principalities and powers. They maneuver to block the flow of God's glory from coming to us. Fallen angels and demons don't have access in the Kingdom of Heaven but have access into the Kingdom of God, which is how satan could accuse Job in the Court *(Job 1:6)* (Courts discussed later).

Don't let any of that scare you, as we already covered who you are with God in this chapter. We are seated with Christ in the Heavenly places in authority. They are scared of you!

God is calling His children, to come out of the wilderness into the Promised Land. He is calling His children to cross over into their supernatural inheritance beyond the veil to take their place in Heaven and take their Seat of Government now and conquer their mountains. He is calling His children into deeper levels of intimacy to see Father and Jesus face to face.

Our Mountains

While operating in the spiritual realm, look for your mountains. We have seven mountains and seven thrones that we need to occupy:

- Personal
- Family
- Work
- Ministry
- Art and entertainment
- Financial
- Ecclesia

These mountains represent our governmental positions of authority. When we occupy our personal mountain, our governmental position, we can rule all the other mountains from there and begin to see our life transform.

Associated with these mountains and thrones are scrolls, decrees, mandates, and resources that we can rest upon. If we are not sitting on them, dragons (satan's principalities) most certainly are and they need to be dethroned. Each person needs to conquer their own mountains. Jesus can help you conquer all the dragons on all seven mountains.

While on your personal mountain, engage with your angel to ask him for your Destiny Scroll.

Sitting on your Throne

In Christ, we are manifest saints and royal-priests sitting on our thrones at the right hand of the Father right now. If you allow God to mold you in His hands and to train you to develop your spiritual senses, to see, smell, touch, feel and taste in the supernatural realm, you will accomplish many victories for the Kingdom of God, build many treasures in Heaven *(Matthew 16:19-21)* and find fulfillment and success, under God's will, in your life now.

We were taught by leaders in the man-made, church-system to sit in pews (not our thrones) and be under someone's covering and when you die, only then will Heaven be revealed. This is religious fantasy that prevents you from fulfilling your destiny.

Your role is not just to engage this earthly realm. God the Father wants to reveal your role in Heaven to you today and every day and for you to take responsibility for your Seat of Government in Heaven.

Crucifixion of the flesh is vital and necessary to happen in one's life in order to move forward in your destiny with God.

Engaging God in the supernatural realm gives you a sense of responsibility and fulfilment in the Heavenly realms. Then you become a gate from Heaven to flow down to earth and bring all that the Father entrusts you to do.

Don't be discouraged if all this sounds overwhelming or if you run into hindrances or nay-sayers. Stay focused and keep at it. It takes time to become mature children of God.

Michael Van Vlymen mentions in his book, "Supernatural Transformation", "You can absolutely live in the spiritual realm and the natural realms with consciousness awareness of both. If that is your desire you can have it. Not only you can have it, God will give you the grace to experience this as normal. There will be an adjustment period but as you grow, you will become comfortable being who you were created to be."

CHAPTER 5
WHAT CROWNS ARE YOU WEARING?

We just discussed sitting on your mountains and your thrones. You need to be in charge of all areas of your life, under God's perfect will, physically and spiritually. While on your journey with God, you need to be wearing certain crowns. Many are available to you.

Most self-professed Christians only wear one crown-the wrong one!

The Bible mentions eight crowns, six of them that we should wear. The Bible says that once a person confesses that Jesus is their only Savior, they become born-again into life; spiritual life. They become a royal priest *(1 Peter 2:9)*, a saint *(Ephesians 2:18-20)*, a child of God and a joint-heir with Jesus *(Romans 8:17)*. One of the capabilities as this new creature in Christ *(2 Corinthians 5:17)*, is, that we have access to God *(Ephesians 2:18)* in Heaven *(Hebrews 10:19)*.

We have the capability to have supernatural encounters with God the Father, Jesus, the Holy Spirit, angels, Heavenly visits, spiritual gifts, miracles, signs and wonders. Yet most Christians have no encounters in or with the supernatural realm.

Why is that?

Much of the blame can be placed on religion. As mentioned, most Christians wallow in the swamps of flesh-operated, religious activities that block spiritual encounters and relationships with God. Most professed Christians are content with this religious-church arrangement, allowing others to occupy their thrones and wear their crowns.

Some have experienced supernatural encounters, but continue to mix the Kingdom's wealth with religion, becoming more of a mongrel Christian that is neither hot nor cold. *"I know your works, that you are neither cold nor hot. I could wish you were cold or hot. So then, because you are lukewarm, and neither cold nor hot, I will vomit you out of My mouth." Revelation 3: 15-16 NKJV*

Some others have made great strides with God in the supernatural, yet lost their Kingdom crowns or deliberately took them off.

So, what are these Kingdom crowns that we should be wearing?

In *Revelation 4:10-11* we are shown, *"the twenty-four elders fall down before Him who sits on the throne and worship Him who lives forever and ever, and cast their crowns before the throne, saying: "You are worthy, O Lord, to receive glory and honor and power; For You created all things, and by Your will they exist and were created." NKJV*

Crowns are symbols that represent our position in the realm of Kingdom government.

God wants us to wear our crowns. Without the crowns, there is no symbol of the recognition of the government in the realm of the Spirit. Each crown gives us more rulership and more access. Whatever we carry in the Kingdom is who we are in the spirit realm. If we are seen by spiritual creatures, such as principalities or demons, wearing the wrong crown or no crowns, what can we expect to be their response when we pray for relief or if we attack them?

Crowns give us rulership in the spiritual and physical realms.

What else do these crowns do?

1. The provision of the reverent crown- it represents a mandate to do a specific job. Crowns represent rulership of the circumstances that come against us in our lives.

2. Crowns are identification of what we carry in the realm of the spirit. Each crown has a specific identity; this identity can release the power of God on our behalf.

3. The spirit world knows what you look like, the same way that we can be identified in the natural realm by people. We each have a different look. In the spirit realm, you can look powerless and weak or powerful and mighty.

"Then I turned to see the voice that spoke with me. And having turned I saw seven golden lamp stands, and in the midst of the seven lamp stands One like the Son of Man, clothed with a garment down to the feet and girded about the chest with a golden band. His head and hair were white like wool, as white as snow, and His eyes like a flame of fire; His feet were like fine brass, as if refined in a furnace, and His voice as the sound of many waters; He had in His right hand seven stars, out of His mouth went a sharp two-edged sword, and His countenance was like the sun shining in its strength." Revelation 1:12-16 NKJV

When we wear Heavenly crowns and are walking in rulership, you and I are likened to Jesus Christ. That is why the enemy many times backs off when you're wearing the crowns from God, because they know what's going to happen to them if they stay or if they fight you. Satan doesn't want us wearing our crowns from God. He will steal our crowns, convince us to take them off or give us a replacement crown. The devil wants to shut down the open Heaven for us to communicate with and have relationship

61

with the Father; hinder our prayer life and stop the worship of God in our lives. All of those three things release spiritual anointing in our lives.

Isaiah 10:27 says that the anointing breaks the yoke of the enemy. The anointing creates Heavenly encounters. We obtain and increase our anointing from salvation, individual anointing, and corporate anointing (groups of mature believers gathered together), with anointing from the Holy Spirit.

Six Crowns we should Carry

Crown of Righteousness

"Finally, there is laid up for me the crown of righteousness, which the Lord, the righteous Judge, will give to me on that Day, and not to me only but also to all who have loved His appearing." 2 Timothy 4:8 NKJV

When we walk under the ways of God with the Holy Spirit, this crown is ours. It is in Christ Jesus that we have righteousness.

Crown of Life

"Blessed is the man who endures temptation; for when he has been approved, he will receive the crown of life which the Lord has promised to those who love Him." James 1:12 NKJV

Rejecting the ways of the world, the ways of religion and denying self daily for the love of Jesus gives us this crown.

Crown of Glory

"Shepherd the flock of God which is among you, serving as overseers, not by compulsion but willingly, not for dishonest gain but eagerly; nor as being lords over those entrusted to you, but being examples to the flock; and when the Chief Shepherd appears, you will receive the crown of glory that does not fade away." 1 Peter 5:2-4 NKJV

Rather self explanatory. When a professed Christian, especially a leader, represents the true Gospel of God to others, this crown is awarded. When they act as religious "bosses" under strange doctrines *(Romans 16:17-18; Hebrews 13:9; 2 Peter 3:17),* they will be judged accordingly.

Incorruptible Crown

"Do you not know that those who run in a race all run, but one receives the prize? Run in such a way that you may obtain it. And everyone who competes for the prize is temperate in all things. Now they do it to obtain a perishable crown, but we for an imperishable crown." 1 Corinthians 9: 24-25 NKJV

We need to strive towards God, towards your destiny with Him, towards an uncompromising, surrendered life to God.

Crown of Rejoicing

"For what is our hope, or joy, or crown of rejoicing? Is it not even you in the presence of our Lord Jesus Christ at His coming? For you are our glory and joy." 1 Thessalonians 2:19-20 NKJV

Winning other souls for Christ.

Crown of Anointing Oil

"Neither shall he go out of the sanctuary, nor profane the sanctuary of his God; for the crown of the anointing oil of his God is upon him: I am the Lord." NKJV

When we come into the presence of God in an intimate way, He gives us this crown.

Al and I have been many times in God's presence. He has given each of us this crown, other crowns, along with robes, scepters and our thrones. The enemy especially wants to keep this crown away from people or to steal it if they have it, as it carries so much. God gives us our crowns, but the enemy, the world or the flesh, can take us out of the Kingdom authority, if we move to follow an alternate kingdom. We can maintain our crowns, through commitment to God, under the Holy Spirit's fresh anointing, worship and encounters with Him.

Our foolish decisions to follow the world's ways; religious ways; a false leader's ways; or ways of self, are personal decisions to remove the crowns of God that are upon us or could come upon us. Satan also wants us to stop our anointing and steal our crowns. You need to take back your crowns if they are lost, discarded or stolen.

How can you Recognize that your Crown was Stolen or you lost it?

There are three main ways your crowns are removed: One by submitting to the hand of man; one by yielding to sin and the other by casting it away.

Revelation 3:11 says, "Behold, I am coming quickly! Hold fast what you have, that no one may take your crown." NKJV

When you submit to someone else or to a religion (go under their spiritual authority or covering as many refer to it), you have willingly handed your crowns away. It's your decision to yield to another rather than to God.

Lamentations 5:16 says, *"The crown has fallen from our head. Woe to us, for we have sinned!" NKJV*

Involvement in sin removes your crown. Statistical research indicates that most people who consider themselves Christian around the world, actually live in sin and have therefore, lost their crowns, if they ever had them.

Psalm 89:39 says, *"You have renounced the covenant of Your servant; You have profaned his crown by casting it to the ground." NKJV*

People cast their crowns away by deliberately disobeying, compromising with, ignoring or in ignorance, reject God's Word, either in thought, word or deed.

All of these ways result in a loss of rulership. With loss of your crowns, you lose the Heavenly river flow of the anointing upon your life. Your capability to operate in the supernatural becomes corrupted and closed off.

Wrong responses to circumstances are another way that crowns are removed from our lives.

Trauma and shock are areas where your crowns can be lost.

The devil knows if you carry your crowns, because when you do, he doesn't have authority over your life, because you are subject to and of another Kingdom.

It's our job to hold on to our crowns.

How can you Recover your Crown?

Have you noticed that your anointing is gone or perhaps Heaven is closed off to you now?

Maybe things in life are going the wrong way.

Or, you and your ministry aren't operating in the supernatural any more.

All of this can be because you have lost your crowns. If someone has taken your crown (you allowed it), you've sinned and lost it or threw it away for some reason, how do you get them back?

Repent for allowing your crown(s) to be removed from your head. Pray in tongues so your spirit connects with God to find answers of what you did that allowed this to happen and where your crown(s) can be recovered.

Ask the Holy Spirit to show you where you lost a particular crown. You may have given them to a corrupt "church" group or to a false leader; whose wrong advice you took or perhaps a friend or relative convinced you to follow a different path from God.

Repent for any sin. You must own you own sin. Restore and put your crown(s) back on.

Go in the spirit as led by the Holy Spirit to retrieve it/them where He knows it/them was removed. If you can't operate with your spiritual senses, then operate by faith and pray for restoration of thecrown(s). Then rebuild your position in worship, commitment to and personal relationship with God.

Crowns are symbols of rulership and the anointing is the power to do the job.

The Crown of Pride

"Woe to the crown of pride, to the drunkards of Ephraim, whose glorious beauty is a fading flower which is at the head of the verdant valleys, to those who are overcome with wine! Behold, the Lord has a mighty and strong one, like a tempest of hail and a destroying storm, like a flood of mighty waters overflowing, which will bring them down to the earth with His hand. The crown of pride, the drunkards of Ephraim, Will be trampled underfoot; and the glorious beauty is a fading flower Which is at the head of the verdant valley, Like the first fruit before the summer, Which an observer sees; He eats it up while it is still in his hand." Isaiah 28:1-4 NKJV

This is the crown we should reject at all cost. The crown of pride is the most prevalent crown among professed Christians, especially leaders. Leaders, who wrestle for worship, control, power, authority, wealth, position and titles, end up releasing death to themselves and to others who follow them. Many leaders, operating in prideful jealousy, try to manipulate and stop others from operating in their God-given power, authority, position, gifts and ministry. They want to be revered. They say, "You shouldn't be doing that. You should be doing things my way, under my agenda, under my covering."

67

When a person turns from God's direction to someone else, their crown has been stolen. The enemy uses these types of leaders to get rid of other's anointing and crowns. In my personal experience, every mainstream denomination and almost all groups and leaders are governed by crowns of pride.

One recent such group I encountered, that called themselves, "the Joshua generation seers", had leaders who were trying to control, denigrate or dismiss whatever I was saying, seeing and doing in the spirit. They were wearing crowns of pride. The enemy was using them to try to knock off my crowns, particularly my crown of anointing and spiritual warfare. I didn't let that happen.

Unfortunately, others in the group submitted to them, rather than following the Holy Spirit. Confronting them about what they were doing (some of it anti-biblical) didn't alter their behavior. I left them. I pray they repent and recover before it's too late. The enemy will use every tactic and trap (i.e. religious leaders who are aggressive, authoritative, charismatic, kind, sweet, intelligent-sounding or even spiritually-gifted) to convince you to take off or give them your crowns, so you need to be steadfast and stand your ground.

Don't allow it!

Crown of Thorns

"And the soldiers twisted a crown of thorns and put it on His head, and they put on Him a purple robe." John 19:2

Jesus identified with us. He was mocked by man's kingdom (world-Roman Empire and religion Jewish Pharisees and Sadducees and others) of his Kingly realm. He identified with our destruction and the removal of our crowns by sin. Jesus took our identity by wearing the crown of thorns and carried our sin.

He replaces these crowns from false kingdoms with crowns of God's Kingdom, if we'll accept them.

God's crowns enable us on our journey with Him. Our crowns are symbols of rulership that we are destined to rule with Christ in Heavenly places. Wearing these crowns and walking in His anointing identifies you to God and the Kingdom. When you walk in the call of and personal relationship with God, the anointing is given to you to provide you the tools to do the job.

Strive to obtain all of the crowns that God has for you.

If you're not wearing your crowns on your mountains and thrones, then someone or something else is.

If you've lost any crowns, it's your choice to go back, repent, pick them up and keep them where they belong. Or, you can stay the way you are, wearing your crown of pride, operating in the flesh or under someone else's crown of pride, who is governing your destiny.

This is the way of death.

"There is a way that seems right to a man, but its end is the way of death. Proverbs 14:12

Race after and accept the crowns that God has for you.

Walk with Him in Heaven.

Nothing else compares.

Chapter 5

CHAPTER 6
THE SEVEN SPIRITS OF GOD

I went to Heaven where Jesus and Father were by a fountain. Jesus gave me water to drink from His hands. After that we all went to a feast in Heaven. There was a long table with Jesus, Father and angels sitting at the head of the table. There were other angels serving us food and wine.

After the feast, Al and I went to the throne room of Father casting our crowns down. Father gave us new crowns that were silver with gold trim. We all danced on the dance floor. After that Father gave us two scrolls. We took the scrolls to the Court of Angels. We gave the scroll to an angel who took it to a judge to be stamped. After that the judge gave me back the scroll and I ate it. It tasted sweet like honey.

I next went to the bridal chambers and saw the seven Spirits of God enveloping all around me.

Some of the wonderful joys and treasures of Heaven that we can partake of as citizens of Heaven are the Seven Spirits of God.

"And from the throne proceeded lightning, thundering, and voices. Seven lamps of fire were burning before the throne, which are the seven Spirits of God." Revelation 4:5

"And I looked, and behold, in the midst of the throne and of the four living creatures, and in the midst of the elders, stood a Lamb as though it had been slain, having seven horns and seven eyes, which are the seven Spirits of God sent out into all the earth." Revelation 5:6

Isaiah 11:1-2 tells us who the Seven Spirits of God are: ***"Then a Shoot (the Messiah) will spring from the stock of Jesse [David's father], And a Branch from his roots will bear fruit. And the Spirit of the LORD will rest on Him— The Spirit of wisdom and understanding, The Spirit of counsel and might, The Spirit of knowledge and of the [reverential and obedient] fear of the LORD."***

The Seven Spirits of God are our Teachers. They teach us about our personal position, our function and our purpose in the Kingdom of God. Those who have gone to Heaven in the spirit, including myself, have seen the Seven Spirits of God. Besides their different functions, they also reflect different colors.

Red – Spirit of the Lord- mandate for position. This Spirit is about our son-ship and lordship.

Orange- Spirit of Wisdom – equips us for position. You ask Wisdom for guidance. When you go to Wisdom for assistance, you'll receive much broader information. Wisdom also takes you where Heaven's various courts are.

Yellow- Spirit of Understanding- Authorizes you for position.

Green- Spirit of Counsel – Prepares you for position. Helps you go before the courts and before the throne of God.

Blue-Spirit of Might- Reveals to you the position of your personal mountain and your throne.

Indigo- Spirit of Knowledge- Empowers you for position.

Violet –Spirit of the Fear of the Lord – Accountability for position.

Wisdom and Counsel go hand in hand together and you can ask them for direction about a specific need that you have.

One time, when I went to my garden, Jesus said, "Come, let's plant some flowers." So, we planted daisies, some white roses and red roses. When we were done, I looked at Jesus, saying that I wanted to meet the Seven Spirits of God.

Spirit of Wisdom soon appeared wearing an orange veil and gown.

She said, "I am the Spirit of Wisdom. I was at the beginning of creation when Father created Heaven and earth.

I said, "I would like to have more wisdom to make wise decisions in my life."

Wisdom said, "Take this and drink."

I drank an orange liquid from a small, slim, crystal bottle that the Spirit handed to me. Then I saw so many green colors around me.

The Spirit of Counsel appeared. He put a beautiful big chain around my neck with a green gem attached to it.

Next, I met the Spirit of Might, who was all blue. This Spirit gave me a very shiny, blue sword.

After that I met the Spirit of Knowledge- indigo. He came to me and put a scroll in my hand and handed me an indigo-colored bottle, saying, "Drink knowledge." He said, "To you have been revealed, the secrets of the Kingdom of God. You shall have knowledge beyond your understanding to help people in their walk with God."

The Spirit of Understanding arrived, who was in yellow. He gave me a scroll.

From here I went in the spirit into this beautiful room that had violet drapes. I could see beams of light shining throughout the room. The Spirit of the Fear of the Lord said, "Sit down." I sat in a chair and He gave me a small music box. When I opened it, there was a small necklace inside, with a violet stone at the end.

He put it around my neck saying, "The Spirit of the Fear of the Lord shall follow you always."

At the end of my Heavenly visit, I met the Spirit of the Lord. I was in this new place totally surrounded by red, as this Spirit walked all around me. I kneeled as the Spirit put a red crown on my head and gave me a red mantle.

After all of this, I went and sat in my seat of government in Heaven.

God has created us to rule with Him… NOW!

"The Spirit Himself bears witness with our spirit that we are children of God, and if children, then heirs—heirs of God and joint heirs with Christ, if indeed we suffer with Him, that we may also be glorified together." Romans 8:16-17

"But God, who is rich in mercy, because of His great love with which He loved us, even when we were dead in trespasses, made us alive together with Christ (by grace you have been saved), and raised us up together, and made us sit together in the Heavenly places in Christ Jesus," Ephesians 2:4-6

God says that we're supposed to take our throne now.

It's time for every Christians to shake off the world and religion and take their honored position with God.

Seek the Seven Spirits of God to obtain more for yourself and your destiny.

You are a saint, a royal priest, an heir, a lord and citizen of Heaven now.

Your throne is waiting for you!

Chapter 6

CHAPTER 7

WISDOM AND HER HANDMAIDENS

"I wisdom existed from the beginning. I dwell on wisdom heights."

Wisdom has its DNA in all creation. Wisdom is a ruler, a magistrate of Heaven, a Queen that governs the whole realm of the kingdom world and has seven handmaidens.

Spirit of Glory

"If you are censured and suffer abuse [because you bear] the name of Christ, blessed [are you—happy, fortunate, to be envied, with life-joy, and satisfaction in God's favor and salvation, regardless of your outward condition], because the Spirit of glory, the Spirit of God, is resting upon you. On their part He is blasphemed, but on your part, He is glorified." 1 Peter 4:14

Spirit of Holiness

"And [as to His divine nature] according to the Spirit of holiness was openly designated the Son of God in power [in a striking, triumphant and miraculous manner] by His resurrection from the dead, even Jesus Christ our Lord (the Messiah, the Anointed One)." Romans 1:4

Spirit of Truth

"But when He, the Spirit of Truth (the Truth-giving Spirit) comes, He will guide you into all the Truth (the whole, full Truth).

For He will not speak His own message [on His own authority]; but He will tell whatever He hears [from the Father; He will give the message that has been given to Him], and He will announce and declare to you the things that are to come [that will happen in the future]." John 16:13

Spirit of Excellence

"Because an excellent spirit, knowledge, and understanding to interpret dreams, clarify riddles, and solve knotty problems were found in this same Daniel, whom the king named Belteshazzar. Now let Daniel be called, and he will show the interpretation." Daniel 5:12

Spirit of Faith

"Yet we have the same spirit of faith as he had who wrote, I have believed, and therefore have I spoken. We also believe, and therefore we speak, assured that He Who raised up the Lord Jesus will raise us up also with Jesus and bring us [along] with you into His presence." 2 Corinthians 4:13-14

Spirit of Life

"But after three and a half days, by God's gift the breath of life again entered into them, and they rose up on their feet, and great dread and terror fell on those who watched them." Revelation 11:11

Spirit of Promise

"In Him you also who have heard the Word of Truth, the glad tidings (Gospel) of your salvation, and have believed in and adhered to and relied on Him, were stamped with the seal of the long-promised

Holy Spirit." Ephesians 1:13

"For the promise [of the Holy Spirit] is to and for you and your children, and to and for all that are far away, [even] to and for as many as the Lord our God invites and bids to come to Himself." Acts 2:39

Encountering Wisdom

I went to the dance floor and was dancing with Father and later I was dancing with Jesus. After that, Wisdom gave me a necklace. She blew dust over my body and it became very shimmery. She gave me a book also.

Wisdom said, "I will teach you to unlock mysteries. Focus and drink from me."

Wisdom brought me gifts and nudged me to follow her. We walked up some stairs and on the right side was a door. I walked through it to see the Spirit of Holiness who had a shimmery bright veil over her head. She put a crown on my head and gave me a fluorescent-white liquid to drink that went through my body making me translucent, full of light. Holiness also gave me a scroll to eat.

I walked out of the room and followed Wisdom through a corridor. She pointed for me to walk through another door, where the Spirit of Life was. I was in the middle of a beautiful meadow with multicolored flowers of gold, blue, pink, orange, all shades of purple, white and green. There were bees, birds, different animals and all creation was present. The Spirit of Life was pulsating through every living creature here that the Father created. The Spirit of Life looks like bright light with shimmery garments. She gave me a sword that was alive.

She said to me, "You don't need to despair. The Spirit of Life will shine through you like beams of light out towards many people on earth. The Life of Christ will shine through you." The Spirit of Life gave me another sword that had written on it, "Conquer the spirit of death."

I came out of this room and followed the Spirit of Wisdom to the next room to meet the Spirit of Promise. She was dressed in blue, veiled garments. She gave me a wooden box. When I opened it, I took out a scroll that had written on it, "All promises from the Father will come true." After that I ate the scroll. The Spirit of Promise gave me a medallion and a crown of Promise.

I followed Wisdom upstairs and entered the Father's chambers where I encountered the Spirit of Faith. She said you shall have faith to move mountains and change nations. She gave me to drink from a red bottle. "Drink faith," she said.

The next room I entered was the Spirit of Truth. She gave me a belt that had written on it, "The Spirit of Truth." Suddenly, out of my mouth came a sword. The Spirit of Truth said to me, "You shall speak the truth that will change people's lives. Speak the truth in love." I could see myself wearing my full armor. "You shall speak the truth that will conquer nations and destroy the kingdom of darkness."

Next, I met with the Spirit of Excellence. She was enveloping me like waves of a multicolored rainbow. She gave me a crown that had written on it, "Sprit of Excellence." She said, "I am going to teach you to speak with Excellence. Through Excellence you will conquer every obstacle in your life."

I went to encounter Wisdom again in the Father's chambers. She is so calming and relaxing.

I looked at Wisdom who had a veil over her head and body with small lights that shined through with shimmery colors. She gave me to drink a honey-like substance from a vessel. She sat next to me on the couch and opened a box. There were thirty vials full of a fluorescent-colored liquid and I drank them all. The frequency of Heaven was vibrating inside of my body.

Father said, "Encounter Wisdom daily, she will teach you all things, all secrets and mysteries. All that you need to do."

Wisdom said to me, "You are highly favored."

I stepped into her saying, "I desire wisdom to make right choices in every area of my life."

She said, "I will teach you the ancient path of the Father."

God the Father, Yeshiva, angels, Wisdom and I then went to walk in the Garden of Eden. A lion came bringing a scroll. Father took the scroll from the lion's mouth and gave it to me. I put the scroll inside of my belly. I met all my other bodies and they all stepped into me. (We have six bodies, the carnal body, the terrestrial body the one that we travel in the spirit, the spiritual body, the natural body, the Heavenly body and the celestial body).

On your journey with God, look for the seven Spirits of God and the Handmaidens of Wisdom. Obtain from them all that they have to offer to assist you on your journey with God.

Chapter 7

CHAPTER 8

FOUR CHAMBERS OF THE HEART

There are four chambers (spiritual) in your heart that can connect you with Jesus and the Father. These four chambers are important because when Adam and Eve sinned, the river of God was shut off to flow through the four rivers that flow with the glory of God. This river has to be poured out on earth again.

1. The Heart Garden
2. The Dance Floor
3. The Soaking Room
4. The Bridal Chamber

The Heart Garden

Your blood carries the thoughts and intents of your heart. The garden is the realm where the intimacy with Jesus and Father is cultivated. There is a river running through your garden that needs to be cultivated.

My Journey into my Heart Garden

I went in the Spirit where Jesus revealed to me that I have a garden to take care of. Just like Adam and Eve had a garden, you and I each have a spiritual garden to attend to and partake of.

I saw myself walking with Jesus through a beautiful river, both of us barefoot wearing white robes. We stopped and He started washing my face with water and then oil.

After that, holding hands, Jesus and I went and sat in this beautiful meadow with white flowers. We sat down and ate fish and bread. My husband Al joined us. It was such a wonderful scene in the presence of the Lord. Then I asked the Lord if I have a garden with flowers and walls and water?

He said, "Yes you do!"

I closed my eyes in soaking prayer and I saw my beautiful garden with red and white roses and purple flowers. Jesus and I walked on a beautiful paved path where He showed me all the trees that were there: palm, cherry, apple and pine trees.

As we walked and explored the garden, He said to me, "You have work to do. See those three rows of weeds? You need to pull them out."

So, I bent down and started pulling them out. Jesus and some angels helped me to pull all the weeds out. I asked the Lord, "What do all these weeds represent."

He said, "Remember when you asked Me to restore and renew your mind so that all those thoughts from the past will not rule your mind anymore?"

I said, "Yes Lord."

He said, "Those weeds are your thoughts. As you spend time with Me in prayer and soaking with music, I am renewing your mind and restoring your garden." The Lord showed me that I have allowed jackals to live in this place which is why I constantly fought the fight of thoughts that came my way; ideas and imaginations and misinterpretation that created fear and strife in my life.

I like the verse in the Word of God in *Colossians 3: 1-2, "If then you have been raised with Christ [to a new life, thus sharing His resurrection from the dead], aim at and seek the [rich, eternal treasures] that are above, where Christ is, seated at the right hand of God. And set your minds and keep them set on what is above (the higher things), not on the things that are on the earth."*

As we set our minds in worship on the things above we are... **"Transformed (changed) by the [entire] renewal of your mind [by its new ideals and its new attitude], so that you may prove [for yourselves] what is the good and acceptable and perfect will of God, even the thing which is good and acceptable and perfect [in His sight for you]." Romans 12:2**

Adam and Eve gave up their rights in their spiritual garden to satan. It's time for all of us to claim what is rightfully ours and what has been given to us through Jesus. Our garden is our dominion in Second Heaven which is in our sphere of influence. We need to survey our walls, build our fences, plant, arrange, etc.

1. Command our walls to be restored
2. Command our gates to be fortified.
3. Invite the Holy Spirit to be our gate-keeper.
4. Ask the Lord Jesus to dwell in this garden with you and get rid of all unnecessary weeds, dry branches, evil spirits, etc.
5. Rest, enjoy, renew and be at peace in your garden, which reflects into your entire life. As you exercise your spiritual mind by setting your mind above, you are setting your mind on the garden and God will bring radical transformation by the renewing of your mind.

Isaiah 35 talks about the Garden: ***"THE WILDERNESS and the dry land shall be glad; the desert shall rejoice and blossom like the rose and the autumn crocus. It shall blossom abundantly and rejoice even with joy and singing. The glory of Lebanon shall be given to it, the Excellency of [Mount] Carmel and [the plain] of Sharon. They shall see the glory of the Lord, the majesty and splendor and Excellency of our God. Strengthen the weak hands and make firm the feeble and tottering knees. Say to those who are of a fearful and hasty heart, Be strong, fear not! Behold, your God will come with vengeance; with the recompense of God He will come and save you. Then the eyes of the blind shall be opened, and the ears of the deaf shall be unstopped. Then shall the lame man leap like a hart, and the tongue of the dumb shall sing for joy. For waters shall break forth in the wilderness and streams in the desert. And the burning sand and the mirage shall become a pool, and the thirsty ground springs of water; in the haunt of jackals, where they lay resting, shall be grass with reeds and rushes. And a highway shall be there, and a way; and it shall be called the Holy Way. The unclean shall not pass over it, but it shall be for the redeemed; the wayfaring men, yes, the simple ones and fools, shall not err in it and lose their way. No lion shall be there, nor shall any ravenous beast come up on it; they shall not be found there. But the redeemed shall walk on it. And the ransomed of the Lord shall return and come to Zion with singing, and everlasting joy shall be upon their heads; they shall obtain joy and gladness, and sorrow and sighing shall flee away."***

Getting to your Garden

Put on some soft worship, instrumental music, lay comfortably on the floor, couch or bed, close your eyes, picture Jesus and ask Him to take you in the spirit to your garden.

Soaking is not worship, praise, speaking in tongues, praying or doing anything but letting God love you and take you in the spirit.

In my garden are beautiful flowers, rabbits, fruit trees... one person told me his garden is an entire planet that has trees that each contain multiple kinds of fruit!

You can also speak words of creation in your garden.

Taking possession of your garden changes the way we think, the way we react to things. It changes the atmosphere around us, as we are opening Heaven above the earth. Once we become born-again, spirit-filled children of God, we need to take dominion of this place. More and more I take dominion over my garden and I become a faithful steward to care for that which God has given me. I find my thoughts being cleaned and cleared up giving me a very sound mind, as I'm not operating in the mind of the flesh anymore, but in the mind of the Spirit. I came to a greater place of awareness of God's presence as I spent time in the intimacy with God in the garden.

Another Journey with Jesus in my Heart Garden

Another journey is when I went in the spirit and was sitting on a rock next to Jesus by a waterfall. I was leaning on His shoulder and asked Him, "What shall we do today Lord?"

He said, "Let's go to your garden."

I saw my beautiful garden with calla lilies, roses, pine trees, fruit trees and many more. Jesus cut some of the calla lilies and put them in a vase inside my mansion. I asked if can we go and see Father and Jesus agreed. We both went to the Father's chambers. It had a cozy fireplace with two couches facing each other. Father, Jesus and the Holy Spirit were sitting across from us. We were surrounded by guardian angels. Father handed me a scroll. I said, "What is written on this scroll?"

He said, "Your destiny." After that I saw Father giving three scrolls to Al. There were two warrior angels standing next to me and a new white horse with a beautiful long mane. His name is Elijah. We were then transported to a high mountain and in the distance, we saw a village in a valley. It was somewhere in Africa where a principality, a black dragon, was flying over the village. There was a lot of witchcraft, witchdoctors, diseases and evil things in this village. We were getting the strategy from the Father on how to take out this dragon. We flew in the spirit towards this dragon. Al and I were on our horses. The dragon turned its head and threw flames at us. The warrior angels blocked the flames with their shields, which projected the fire back at the dragon's head. It jerked and moved away from us. Many angels threw ropes around its head and body to hold it still. Al flew on Whitey (his horse), pulled his long sword out and cut its head off. When the dragon fell into the valley, black blood came out of its belly. There were also huge diamonds and purple vials lying around. I put some of the diamonds and vials in my bag.

After that Jesus, Al and I went to heal sick people in the village. I took the vials out, gave them to drink and they all got healed from their diseases. Al started to teach people about spiritual warfare. While Al was teaching, I healed the sick: a man without a leg received a new leg, a blind girl received her sight and a deaf man received his hearing. When all was done, we went back to Father's chambers to fellowship by the fireplace. Angels were giving us cookies. It was awesome.

Father gave each of us a box. Al opened his gift. There were lots of scrolls, a dagger with a silver handle, a sword, and a case that held a bow and arrows.

The last gift inside was a chain with a locket at the end. Al put it around his neck.

I opened my gift box. There was a necklace inside with a light-green gem on it. After that, angels took us to the corner of the room where there was a huge bath. Then, it was like the flesh from our bodies opened up like a zipper. We both sat in our spirit bodies in this tub as angels purified us with oil and fire. They gave us new robes and priestly garments, put crowns on our heads, scepters in our hands and we went and sat on our mountain of authority.

Father said, "You've been purified and washed clean, stay on the narrow path. You are rulers in my kingdom; you've been given a galaxy to rule. Guard your heart and your mind. Trust Me, I Am!"

Praise God for this victory! To Him is all the glory.

The Dance Floor Chamber

The dance floor is a place of embracing in love, the presence of the Lord.

The first artery that flows from your heart goes into your brain and the rest of your body. The blood that has the most oxygen gets to the brain first. It carries the thoughts and intents of your heart to program your mind to think in certain ways. So, whatever captures your heart will reflect your thinking. We must be careful not to let our heart be influenced by the world or demons, but only by the Holy Spirit

I went to the dance floor which was of white marble. I was wearing my golden royal robes and had my crown on. Jesus and I danced in a Mozart-style dance. One step forward touching one hand at a time and doing pirouettes. Father joined us and we all danced in a small circle and turned in twirls. I saw the seven Spirits of God weaving around us, with rainbow colors. Then I saw an angel playing the flute, who was wearing a white robe. A lion came on the floor and was weaving among us. Jeremiah came and brought a golden shimmery light scroll. On the scroll was written: "It's time to unite and come up higher."

The Bridal Chamber

It is the bridegroom's job to prepare the bridal chambers. We need to become unified in body, soul and spirit with Jesus Christ. There is a level of union with the presence of the Father that we need to come to as sons and daughters of God, to be able to become co-heirs with Him. Our character is crucial as it holds the testimony of God and holds a reservoir of the presence of the Lord that empowers us to be able to stand in difficult circumstances. The earth will not respond to us unless we are seated in Heaven.

I went in the spirit to the bridal chambers and saw a very bright light. Jesus gave me a crown of light that was very shimmery adorned with white diamonds. I was wearing white garments and a white robe. Jesus also gave me a honey-like substance to drink. I kept drinking for a while, and then my body suddenly became very shimmery. I received a bigger emerald green jar to heal the sick. After that I went to sit on my seat of authority.

I also received an orange robe and a crown. Jesus put a precious stone around my neck, we went dancing and Father also came in. I met Kathryn Kuhlman who gave me a scroll. We went to the Father's chambers by the fireplace where angels brought us cookies. After that I went to the weapon room and met my warrior angels there. One of them gave me a green and a red sword which I used to kill a dragon in the spirit.

I went back to the bridal chambers and saw a bright light. Jesus gave me a crown that was white-shimmery and sparkling with diamonds. He also gave me a honey-like substance to drink, which made my entire body become very bright light. I then sat on my seat of authority.

The Soaking Room Chamber

This is where the preparation of the bride takes place with many fragrances and incense. Queen Esther spent a year being soaked in oils and spices, to prepare for her wedding. The soaking room of preparation in our heart is directly connected with our marriage with Jesus Christ.

The soaking room was a spa-like room where angels were holding towels and trays with fragrances. Bath oils were all around the room. I entered the room and laid down in this big tub. One at a time the angels poured all the fragrances into the water… orange peels, frankincense, lavender, cinnamon, lemon, honey, a shimmery-white liquid, etc. After soaking, I received orange garments and an orange robe. I was wearing an orange-colored crown that had ornate rubies and diamonds. I was brought into a room where Jesus was waiting for me. We went back to the dance floor and danced. Father joined us.

I want to carry the fragrance of Jesus Christ on the earth.

These are just a few examples of my experiences to the four chambers of my heart. I share many more later that blend in with various, amazing adventures that I encountered on my journey with God.

Chapter 8

CHAPTER 9

GETTING JUSTCE IN THE MOBILE COURT

Did you know that any injustice that happened to you in your life can be taken to the courts of Heaven? As we have courts of justice here on earth there are courts in Heaven where you can go and receive justice. If you have repeatedly been robbed or cheated by the devil for most of your life, or you have a disease that has not been healed for a long time, you can go before the throne of God and present your case. The cloud of witnesses will be there also.

Great isn't it?

How can you go to the Courts of Heaven?

1. Pray that God will open your eyes in the spirit to see the mystery of His Word and His glory. In the glory there is no time and space and there is no distance in the glory.

2. Before you go to the Throne of God make sure you have repented of any sin, broken curses, removed wrong people from your life (you probably missed something, which is why you're going to court to find out what right the accuser has against you).

3. Ensure that your mountains, thrones, crowns, four chambers of your heart are under your authority (if possible).

4. Soak or be still with some worship music and ask the Holy Spirit to take you to see in the spirit.

5. Ask God to give you this ability.

Once you start seeing with your spiritual sight, you'll see pictures that appear in your mind, assisted by the Holy Spirit, of what's taking place in Heaven's courts.

When you go to the courts of Heaven you can see the Judge – God the Father on His chair/throne, Jesus as your lawyer and satan as the accuser. You can present your case before God the Father and as you repent of all your specific sins you can have the confidence that you will win!

The accuser of the brethren will say that you deserve punishment or that they have the right to attack you because you're a sinner, but you can argue your case is covered with the blood of Jesus and repentance which brings forgiveness or justification of your case to be won. Jesus will declare that you are innocent before the court.

Job argued his case in the courts of Heaven, pleading to go straight to the Judge of Heaven and earth: *"But I desire to speak to the Almighty and to argue my case with God" Job 13:3.* And Job continues saying, *"Even though he kills me, I'll trust him. At least I'll be able to argue my case to His face."*

"God stands up to open Heaven's court..." Psalm 82:1

Most Christians lose battles on earth because they don't have the knowledge of showing up to the courts of Heaven- they lose by default.

"My people are destroyed for lack of knowledge." Hosea 4:6

We need to get revelation knowledge of God, knowledge of the glory that can unlock the realms of Heaven.

Just like a crafty lawyer on earth, the devil is a legalist and tries to find a loophole against you. And he will find a loophole if you have not repented of areas that he can use against you. You must ask God to forgive you of all sin and cleanse you with the Blood of Jesus, before you go to the court of Heaven. Any you've missed, the devil will bring up in court, and so, you can handle it there.

There are several reasons we can engage the mobile court such as:

- To remove blockages, evil strongholds keeping us from our destiny
- To remove a disease
- To resolve legal, family or financial problems
- To be delivered from principalities, powers, demons

If a demon has a legal right to your life it will not cooperate with Jesus. Repentance is vital in this case, because satan accuses God's children day and night and if we don't live a righteous life, he will have a legal right to attack us in many different ways.

Here's a testimony given to me in the mobile court case of a brother who the enemy stole from him all of his life of jobs, possessions, relationships, etc.:

As he went to the court of Heaven, God the Father was the judge sitting on the throne, Jesus was his advocate and the devil's advocate was the accuser. This brother repented and covered himself with the blood of Jesus as he presented his case before the Lord.

He said, "Before I went to court, I repented and forgave all who had hurt me and wronged me and asked God to forgive them and me for all my sins." The brother pled his case, smashing his fist on the table in front of him to emphasise the crimes that had been done against him.

The accuser angrily said, "I have a right to steal from him, as he was a fornicator and a liar."

Jesus said, "It's all covered by My Blood. Release all that you stolen back to him."

The accuser said, "No."

Then the Judge spoke. Father Judge said to the court and to the brother, "All funds are released. All dry river beds now will flow with milk and honey. Joy, love, peace and harmony is restored. Restlessness is taken away and bound. Prosperity is released. Calm is restored. Spiritual alignment is put back in place and healing upon him is restored. Faith and understanding flows into him now."

Next, a teaching mantle was handed to this brother and a cup to drink from which was power (he was informed). A spear was handed to him to slay unrighteousness. The accuser was gagged and dragged away in chains out of the court by two angels. The Holy Spirit was also standing there next to Jesus in the shape of a man that looked like a combination of water, light and sparkling water (hard to explain).

Its one thing to forgive someone for not being honest and stealing from you, but it's another thing to take your "adversary" to the mobile courts of Heaven to get him to pay back what is owed to you or what has been blocked from reaching you. You can go after what was stolen in the spiritual realm that affected the physical realm, to obtain a verdict forcing the devil to release and return. This also works when we're being treated unfairly or unjustly by people in circumstances in life. Take the situation to God's court and present your case.

The Mystic Love of God

Justin Abraham said, "The entire mystic realm flows through love of God the Father, Jesus the Son and the Holy Spirit. One of the things that stop the love of the Father is when you feel disappointed or hurt or whatever you are going through. The cares and the worries of this world choke the seed and that is why we don't need to be mystical in this case but we let God the Father touch our heart at a deeper emotional level.

Sometimes your court case in Heaven isn't effective because your heart is wounded. What you need to do is let Yeshua minister to you. It is the Father's good pleasure to give you the Kingdom. By faith, step in and get anchored in God's goodness. Experience the multidimensional facets of His love. Ascend into the light into dimensions of His love."

Justin Abraham also said, "A mystical person is someone who thinks in their heart that:

- He restores my heart
- He makes me lie down in green pastures
- He fills my cup
- Mystical people are slaves of love
- They allow God to manifest through them
- Now He is taking me inside the House of Wine, makes me drunk with His kisses
- For your sweet love is better than wine. Let him kiss you with the kisses of his mouth. For your love is better than wine *(Solomon 1:2).*
- A non-mystic person is one who fights being in love with Him
- A mystic person is someone who is enlarged with His love."

Many Christians go to God for things but they don't always get results. If you need healing then you must go to God as the Healer. If you need love you go to God as the Father. Most Christians get the healing, forgiving and love from God part, but when it comes to justice, they ignore that part.

We need to go to God the Judge when we need Him as Judge. He can judge your case on your behalf and bring justice.

The court of Heaven is always open!

No appointment needed!

Cleaning Gateways in the Spirit

There are many gateways of body, soul and spirit that need to be cleansed after we received Jesus Christ as our saviour. When we spend time in the presence of God our spirit man is renewed daily. This is a lifetime process and it pertains to our inner life.

The Spirit has the following gateways: revelation, intuition, reverence, faith, hope worship and fear of God.

Soul has: conscience, reason, imagination, mind, emotion choice and will.

The body has: touch, taste, smell, sight and hearing.

Depending on what people have been involved in such as trauma, witchcraft, sexual immorality, heretical religion, etc., it gives legal rights to demons to control gateways because we have yielded to sin. Repentance and cleansing gateways daily is vital for every believer to be successful in their walk with god.

Jesus and I next went through my body gateway. I saw a familiar spirit abusing my physical body with a whip. Warrior angels took it out immediately and chained it.

Through each of these processes, shadows, which were evil spirits, came out of my subconscious gateway, were taken in chains to the mobile court in Heaven to be judged by God the Father.

I went in the spirit to the Father's throne room. He was sitting on the throne that was a bright, light almost blinding me. I cast my crown before Him and He came down and put the crown back on my head.

He said, "My precious daughter, my precious flower come."

I said, "Father put me on the altar please."

Father took my body and threw it on the altar. The fire intensified more and more as I was purified on the altar.

After that Jesus and I went to my body's gateways. We opened the door to the subconscious gateway. Inside it was dark but as I looked at the walls, I saw many boxes inside the wall. Jesus took a box on the left and when He opened it, out came many familiar spirits in the form of flies. Familiar spirits were attached to memories in the past regarding physical abuse that I went through years ago. My identity was attacked many times in the past by people who defiled me and called me names, because of where I was born. My nervous system was trapped because of it and it was picking up the frequency of those negative memories. Warrior angels caught all the flies in a small net and burned them.

Jesus then took a fiery scroll that also had a new dimension of light in it, and placed it in the wall where the box was.

Beams of light were illuminating now from this part of the wall.

Jesus took out a second box that had worms in it. These familiar spirits and fragments were attached to the mental and emotional abuse done by my mother. The angels took a torch and burned them all to a crisp. Amen! After this, Jesus took another fiery scroll and put it in the wall. The light from it was bigger than the first one.

When Jesus opened a third box, bugs flew out. Other familiar spirits were attached to the mental and emotional abuse done to me where I had attended College. My warrior angels burned them also. Jesus took a fiery scroll and put it in the wall and the light became bigger than the second one.

The fourth box that Jesus took out was black and out of it came snakes and lizards. My warrior angels immediately took them in sacks and brought them to the courts. Jesus took a fiery scroll and placed it in the empty shelf. This light became very powerful illuminating the entire gate. I was set free. Praise God!

Mobile Court Session

In the court, Jesus was my advocate and God the Father was the judge. The devil was the advocate for all the evil spirits that were lined up waiting for the sentence. I saw myself in chains with shackles from both wrists and ankles. Suddenly the shackles fell off and I was standing next to Jesus.

Jesus looked at the evil spirits and shouted, "No more, you've done enough damage. Let her go."

The devil said, "I have a right to accuse her."

Jesus said, "No," as he unrobed himself showing His scars, "By My stripes she is healed and set free. You have neither right nor access to my child."

I repented for all the unforgiveness that I was dwelling on.

Jesus approached the bench where God the Father was. Father said, "No more. You are sentenced to death."

He then gave a scroll to Jesus and He placed it in my hand. My warrior angels took the evil spirits out of the court and threw them in the lake of fire.

PRAISE GOD FOR VICTORY IN JESUS NAME! FREEDOM!

I then went to my heart garden and walked with Jesus in the river. He poured water all over my head and body and said, "You are purified, made clean. Be steadfast in Me, remain in my peace."

Here is a testimony of a court case against Lydia from South Africa that I presented on her behalf.

Lydia's testimony to me:

"I don't know who to ask. Hope you don't mind me sharing my dream? I don't trust anyone else with it. Can you maybe explain? Why am I having this type of dream? Is something wrong with me spiritually? I know I only serve one God no other. I experienced no fear. But in this dream, I was collected from my house by this black being (most definitely not an angel from the Lord). It took me on a horse to the woods where I was handed over to the leader, also on a horse.

Don't know how many there were on three horses, but they are made of black bones (horses included), with red fire amongst the openings of these bones. The leader took me and poked a long-clawed finger in my side. Then I was returned back home. What is going on?

The Lord is busy revealing that I should clean my bloodline which I have been doing. But last week one of our intercessors said that I am not receiving what God wants to give me because there is something like a black veil over me. Ever since then, I've sat before the Lord in prayer as He leads.

What is happening? I have also sensed, when praying in the spirit, a pentagram. I kept on praying.

There is also a lightness and release of healing since I have been seeking the Lord. But now this dream? It doesn't make sense?"

I asked Father for scripture explaining the dream, "Please can you shed some light on this dark matter?"

I went to the mobile court on behalf of Lydia and this is what I saw:

There was generational iniquity in her bloodline that had not be dealt with or repented of on behalf of her ancestors. In **Deuteronomy 5:9** God visits the iniquity from generation to generation... ***"for I, the Lord your God, am a jealous God, visiting the iniquity of the fathers upon the children to the third and fourth generations of those who hate Me..."***

God the Father was the judge, Jesus Christ was the lawyer and the accuser at the left corner was accusing Lydia.

I was taken somewhere else where the accuser had her bound with chains: one big metal collar with a big chain, then chains on each arm and leg. There was witchcraft in Lydia's bloodline and that is why she was chained. While there, Lydia confessed her generational iniquity on behalf of her ancestors.

After that I turned to the accuser and said, "Let her go."

Jesus had warrior angels surround a black creature that said, "She is guilty. She has sinned."

Jesus said, "She has repented. Now let her go."

The creature didn't want to let her go. A fireball came from Heaven and hit this creature, smashing it to the ground, destroying it.

Jesus took Lydia inside the court. She had no chains on now. Angels took sponges and washed her with water and Jesus gave Lydia a clean, white robe and anointed her with oil.

Result… Lydia went in prayer before the Lord and said that she saw the dark veil lifting from her. She has been set free and healed. Amen!

PRAISE GOD FOR THE VICTORY!

Another Victory in the Mobile Court of Accusation

Before I was going to the courts on my own, I'd asked assistance from a few groups that said they assisted people in the courts. Doing this can bring results, depending on who you work with, but can also be dangerous, as you'll see.

This first court session is a court session that I went through with a group of seers. This one is a good example of what can be done with a group.

Court Session 1

Father, we greet You, we honor You, because You are so marvelous. We claim the blood of Yeshua over our lives. We bless Holy Spirit and Yeshua, we welcome You into the courts and we also welcome the Seven Sprits of God, we bless each one of them. Father would you mandate any accuser that has anything against any of us, because we stand together in unity.

This is what they saw in the court:

Seer 1. Incarceration of the mind, I hear "Why can't I go ahead and why am I stuck here?"

Seer 2. Crown of thorns around your head and every time you try to move these thorns, they sink in, keeping you immovable.

Seer 3. I see distorted mirrors.

Seer 4. Witchcraft.

Seer 5. I see ice like stalactites hanging from the courts; very sharp and pointy.

Father we agree with all these accusations. This is generational, coming down through my mother's bloodline where there were lots ofmental, physical trauma and hatred within the family. Father, how many generations back does it go and what was the root cause?

Seer 1. I see a dark forest and the trees were very dark, with no leaves and I see red inside the forest.

Seer 2. There was woman that was abandoned and left to raise children by herself going through hardship. This woman was experiencing a curse.

Seer 3. I saw war and I heard the word "war" and it was such an extreme grief that this woman called out for help.

Seer 4. There are roots of bitterness, desperation and lots of anger towards God and kids.

Seer 1. I see trauma.

Seer 2. I see a young man that was carrying a lot of the load and there is harshness and no affection.

Seer 3. There is a disease that keeps traveling within the family and it was like nausea, the turning of insides, spirit of infirmity. Its DNA that Father doesn't want.

I see a lot of black and red and this young man is opening the black box and what came out were bats and smoke. Something was opened and I see black and red.

Seer 4. Father, are we dealing with any principalities here? What door was opened?

I see something was wiped out clean but it spawns again and it was cleaned and it spawns again and again.

What door was opened and what was the vow made of the blood covenant?

Seer 1. I see a figure that wears a cloak but I can't see its face and it would wrap this cloak around the entire family and it was a false sense of protection. It comes with a promise to give but it's actually stealing.

Seer 4. Father, would You set this figure in front of Your bench that we may see what it is. I see it. It's like a skeleton and it camouflages itself like a shape-shifter and when you take that cloak off it's just a skeleton with death underneath.

Seer 3. I saw famine. It looked like it was something desirable but when the cloak was ripped open it was empty famine. This skeleton is promising something that it doesn't have.

Seer 5. I hear depression and suicidal thoughts. I see a whole community of people dancing around this skeleton. There is alcohol addiction. The cloak is deception like the tree of good and evil and it wants to project fear into the generation where you are. It wants to project fear so that you will take it with your own hand.

Seer 1. I saw a very long, heavy chain and it binds to all that was mentioned and everyone in that family is carrying this chain. It's a burden but they don't know how to cope with it and they don't want to give it up because it's so a part of them such as familiar spirits. It's a promise that it can't deliver and a hope that is being denied.

Seer 4. Father is this a principality that we are not to touch, that twists and turns? Father, would You gag this thing and sit it at the front underneath Your eye?

Seer 2. I see a black and red dragon that is iridescent-red that is a blood covenant. He is very proud, rebellious and defiant.

Seer 4. Father, when we are done here can You please bind this dragon with the chain that was binding this family.

Seer 5. Another accuser that is revealed though this family blood-line is pride. Attached to it is a rebellion spirit and a legalistic spirit. The dragon was saying, "I will show you how to take care of yourself." There is this constant competition to be right and perfect within the family. And have it all together. It doesn't bring forth life, but death and is feeding from the tree of knowledge of good and evil.

There is another spirit of leviathan that displays chaos, confusion, insanity and murder, deceptions and lies. Father, we ask that You bind it and gag it and put it in front of the bench please.

Seer 5. There is a snake without a head with its tail around you that wiggles around and around you. The snake without the head and tail takes its authority from the red and black dragon

Leviathan is one spirit that we are not supposed to take out with our own hands. Father wants to take care of it.

The dragon and the leviathan are two parts of the demonic trinity. Because satan is the head and the leviathan and the dragon take the other two positions.

We are going to agree with all the accusations in court right now. Father, we ask You that You judge us as we stay under the blood of Yeshua and we ask forgiveness.

I saw the gavel in the spirit and I heard Father say, "Not guilty."

Father, I want to ask Rhoda's body in the court to speak out why she is having problems with her skin. (I've had psoriasis on my hands and feet for more than four years).

Because of that snake without a head is why I have had issues with my skin. My skin was red and peeling on my feet.

Father as You have judged us, we ask that You judge these things with the same standard that You have judged us by.

Seer 4. Father, we ask You to bring them to dust so there is nothing left that these things can accuse us of. Father, every trading floor that has been traded in wrongfully, we ask You to bring them to dust, so that the names are removed and all the legal rights are gone. Every agreement and contract and vow that has been made by us and by our generations, even those made in blood, that You will break each and every one of them and consume them with fire. Father, we ask there is no record left for the adversary to work from, we ask that You cut it off. Father, every curse that has been spoken over by us or others we ask that You break it in Jesus name. Father, we ask for every legal right that was used by our adversary to be terminated. Father, we ask that everything that was done here today in court to be washed back in her generational line.

Father, You are the best possible dad that You do things for us that we don't understand. Father, we ask for paperwork reflecting everything that was done in court today.

Father, we ask for complete separation and divorce from any kind of witchcraft and serpent, dragon spirits, from any of them ever coming back to Rhoda's life, unless she invites them in. Father we pray that you keep that door closed that there is no more legal right to ever come back. Father we ask for freedom from the past that has come down on her generational line that has bound her.Father we ask for an outpouring of Your love, that she is so washed in how much You love her, that she drips Your love wherever she goes.

Rhoda. I received two scrolls from the Father. They reflect His goodness and help us to draw closer to Him. I took the scrolls to the Court of Scribes, I recorded them and received two copies. I put the original scroll into my heart and took the two copies to the Court of Angels and handed them to two angels that were behind the counter. I asked them to assign the correct number and ranking of angels to fulfill the scrolls. I commanded my angels to fulfil the mandates of the scroll and to use me as a gateway, because I am a gate. The angels will go into the past, present and future to fulfill the scroll's mandate. I also received a gift from Father and that means there are new things coming to me. I saw a red scroll with gold trim. I saw gold letters coming from the scrolls into me meaning new revelations from Father and more growth to the point that I will look like the Father.

As a result of going to the courts in this session I have received freedom from depression and from suicidal thoughts. For a long time I was harassed by familiar spirits that were tormenting me daily regarding my identity, but with Jesus I prevailed. Praise God for victory!

Court Session 2

In this session I went with the same people I did previously, but this time it was different. A spirit of manipulation and control was governing them. We all went to the Mobile Court...

Sear 1. We start by honoring the court and declare the following, "We greet You Father, You who are Majesty, You are power, You are glory, You are ancient of days and Your Love is ever new. We greet You Yeshua, we greet You Holy Spirit and the Seven Spirits of God.We honor You All. Father we come and stand under the blood of Yeshua as our covering and we ask that You are mandating into the court any and all accusers, who have anything against any of us.

Whenever someone is at the Mobile court of Accusation, several seers can share their input as we collect evidence from the accusers.

Seer 2. I see such an opposite picture than what normally happens in this court. Father is holding you in His embrace and the following accusations are, that you are not loved because you are alone or you are not good enough. I see Father standing between you and those accusations; there is such as awesome awareness of Father's and Yeshua's love of such tenderness towards you and it supersedes any accusations. It is a very safe place to be in the Father's presence.

Seer 3. I understand what Seer 2 is saying because evil spirits are lunging at her and Father wins when they threaten you. I heard the word, "insecure", so the protection of this is pride, but it doesn't come across that way; it's like two sides of a coin. The way I am seeing it is like a false perception. You can't see them but you jump when they are trying to intimidate you or aggravate you or frustrate you. I hear rage aggravating anger, tired, walk a lonely road. People don't understand you and there is

frustration with it, but your heart is saying I wouldn't change it. It means a lot to the Father when you have this attitude but you don't have to put up with those accusations and frustrations.

False-seer 2. I see different jackets and robes and if you put them on you can make it through the day. You put one on and it brings you joy, but they are learned patterns that you are getting your strength in what you put on instead of directly from the Father. You can trust Him to take care of you and you don't have to put on any jackets; He will do the putting on. Part of it is self-sufficiency and that could come as an accusation. All the other ladies said, "I agree."

Seer 4. It could be interpreted as an independent spirit.

Rhoda. I asked them if they still see a snake without a head and tail around me that keeps appearing and disappearing (which they had previously seen).

Seer 3. It's still there but this time it's trying to camouflage itself and be transparent. There is resistance; something is stuck that represents this spirit. It was also saying that I cannot live without it. It is very possible that one of those fragments hang on to this spirit because it believes a lie.

False-seer 1. That could be why you don't want to hear and why you don't want to see because that fragment doesn't want to hear and see the lie that I can't live without it. (This was where they're trying to control, guilt and manipulate me that I didn't want to see and hear, supposedly God, which in reality was their false-doctrines coming out, that was discussed prior to our session to court, that they wanted me to see and hear. Demons are sneaky). Sometimes this is like a protective mechanism that we develop when we go through trauma.

There was a moment or a pause of darkness where Father (they said) was doing something and they couldn't see anything. We were waiting in silence.

111

Seer 3. When Father was standing between you and the accusers He said, "I really love you and I am going to take care of this." But it feels like something inside of you that you don't want to let go of this cushion. This spirit is deceitful and is torturing you, but Father wants to get rid of it.

After we all soaked for a while, Seer 3 says, I see Father's hand around you and in-between this camouflage spirit and it lifted off you and fell to the ground like a jacket that wasn't fitting you anymore. I also heard that you are supposed to turn all things to the Father so that He will take care of it and it will require more faith for you to do this.

Some of the seers then told me that I am not supposed to do spiritual warfare.

More came out of their own minds with demonic influence.

False-seer 2. I have to share something I was going through. I hear this blood curdling scream because of pain. It seems like it was coming out of you Rhoda, a scream, and I saw you fill up with a whole arsenal of swords and spears and axes and that was your defense to take those things to protect yourself. Those weapons were old and the Father was saying just like False-seer 3 was saying (during this the Holy Spirit is telling me, that this is all false) those weapons need to be set aside and you come into the Father. It was such a silencing of the scream and the healing of the scream when you put those weapons away. You know how to use them and that is what is familiar to you and you need to lay them aside.

False-seer 4. Spiritual warfare is redundant.

I ended the session and cut all ties with them.

This is a glaring example of Christian witchcraft with so many tools they were using against me such as guilt, control, manipulation, peer pressure, false words from God, pride, charm and insults.

They believed and were trying to convince me that God's Word on spiritual warfare was not to be done anymore.
It was "old-fashioned", from an "old age" and we're in a "new-age" now they said. Yeah, they have a new age thinking alright.

Not surprising where they were deceived, as they are all ardent followers of a leader who believes such things. Jesus, God the Son, is our template and about one-third of His walk, following only Father's will with the Holy Spirit, was engaged in direct spiritual warfare.

God's Word says, *"For we are not wrestling with flesh and blood [contending only with physical opponents], but against the despotisms, against the powers, against [the master spirits who are] the world rulers of this present darkness, against the spirit forces of wickedness in the heavenly (supernatural) sphere. Ephesians 6:12*

"The sum of Your word is truth [the total of the full meaning of all Your individual precepts]; and every one of Your righteous decrees endures forever." Psalm 119:160

Jesus said, *"Sky and earth will pass away, but My words will not pass away." Matthew 24:35*

God's Word is valid forever. God warns us of people who say otherwise.

For those who say, "Well, they're not all bad. They're just deceived in that area."

That's not sound doctrine from God's Word. Jesus said that even a small amount of false teaching destroys, in God's eyes, all that they do.

"And Jesus [repeatedly and expressly] charged and admonished them, saying, look out; keep on your guard and beware of the leaven of the Pharisees and the leaven of Herod and the Herodians." Mark 8:15

"A little leaven (a slight inclination to error or a few false teachers) leavens the whole lump [it perverts the whole conception of faith or misleads the whole church]." Galatians 5:9

This group was oddly familiar with another group that I was part of and tried to steal my Crown of Spiritual Warfare that God gave me. I thought, "Can this really be really happening again? Can these sweet-sounding ladies really be deceived by evil spirits like the others were?" In all common sense, what other than evil spirits would want spiritual warfare against them to stop?

"But what I do, I will continue to do, [for I am determined to maintain this independence] in order to cut off the claim of those who would like [to find an occasion and incentive] to claim that in their boasted [mission] they work on the same terms that we do. For such men are false apostles [spurious, counterfeits], deceitful workmen, masquerading as apostles (special messengers) of Christ (the Messiah). And it is no wonder, for Satan himself masquerades as an angel of light; So, it is not surprising if his servants also masquerade as ministers of righteousness. [But] their end will correspond with their deeds." 2 Corinthians 11:12-15

Several days later I went to the Father's chambers and we hugged. I went to the throne room and stepped into the Father and His Light filled me up. I asked the Father to show me my Spiritual Warfare Crown that He gave me.

Father said, "You almost lost it again but you prevailed. The enemy tried to steal it from you again. Don't get entangled with foolish ignorant people. They cause disdain in the ministry that I gave you."

I replied, "Yes Father," as I gazed in wonderment at my beautiful purple crown with the huge sapphire in the middle and small rubies all around it. Father put it back on my head. I felt so much peace when I had my crown back. I was wearing my full armor on again, that I wear it when I'm out killing dragons, snakes and other beasts in the spirit.

Bob Jones then walked in and said, "Stay focused on the task Father gave you. Don't be entangled with deceitful people. Focus on writing the book." Bob unwrapped the book (this book that I'm writing now) and showed me how beautiful it is. He continued, "The devil is trying to hinder you and wants to keep you from fulfilling God's destiny that He has for you."

I then saw and heard Father rebuking those false-seers for allowing themselves to be deceived by the enemy, "Your ignorance does not impress me. I Am in this 100% in this and if you are not able to see it and discern then get out of the way. When you come against My child then you come against Me. I Am. I created everything. Don't be blind but get discernment. Repent of your foolishness and ignorance. Repent of your hypocrisy and pride. You are not in charge, I AM. Stop judging what you don't understand. Stay away if you don't accept this ministry."

These people were blinded by evil spirits thinking they were doing me a favor, but they enemy was working through their minds to steal what Father gave me from the beginning. As God's Word warns us over and over, the enemy will sneak in if we are not careful.

Jesus said, *"The thief comes only in order to steal and kill and destroy. I came that they may have and enjoy life, and have it in abundance (to the full, till it overflows)." John 10:10*

The Spirit of Wisdom also cried out to me, "Follow me and discern."

I thank Father God for protecting Me.

I rebuked these women and told them what Father said, but they didn't repent. Not surprising, as few ever turn from their ways even when you point out to them how they are disobeying God's Word. They wear the crowns of pride.

More and more I understand why the desert fathers in Egypt in the fourth century preferred to live alone with God, away from deceitful, religious, prideful, worldly people. Nothing beats walking with the Lord.

CHAPTER 10

TRAVELLING IN THE SPIRIT,
SPIRITUAL WARFARE AND HEALING ECSTASIES

The following are my testimonies of travelling and operating in the spirit (ecstasies) on My Journey with God over the years.

There are times that I spend wonderful moments in Heaven, in Father's throne room or in a spectacular garden or some other almost indescribable spot. Other times I'm in the spirit on earth on various assignments, such as doing spiritual warfare or healing or raising the dead. Many times, we journey to some of the same areas on earth to assist different people. Some of my journeys are a combination of several places and multiple activities.

One of my favorite spots in creation are the cascading waterfalls with suspension bridge that is depicted on the book cover.

The main purpose that God asked me to write this book is to assist you with your own journey with Him.

The testimonies are taken, for the most part, straight out of my journal as I quickly wrote them while it was happening.

When I write my ecstasies, I'm specifically spending quiet time with God at our special place on the beach next to a beautiful lake.

Teaching me how to Write

I asked Jesus to give me a sound mind.

Jesus said, "Declare you have the mind of Christ."

The Lord took me to the library of Heaven that had many books. I saw a huge book opened and Jesus said, "Write."

I said, "Lord teach me how to write."

He said, "You know how to write, there's a small seed inside of you, you just need to develop the seed. Write about your journey with Me. Write about the experiences you have with Me."

My first journey into Spiritual Warfare - Wednesday October 3, 2008

I was on a high rocky mountain riding Isaiah, my horse, wearing my full armor: breast plate, shield of faith, sword, and metal shoes. I was walking on a high cliff, when a huge dragon appeared in front of me, with its mouth open throwing flames at me, which I blocked with my shield. The flames were so big my helmet was getting hot. I reached into a bag of weapons on the right side of Isaiah and pulled out a flame-thrower-type weapon, pointed it at the dragon's head and pressed the button, which blasted out flames, burning the dragon to a crisp. It fell off the mountain into ashes.

Next, I went on my healing mountain where there was a bat-creature hovering over it and when I went to sit on my seat of authority, there was a reptile sitting on my throne. I threw a hammer-weapon at its head, knocking it down to the valley. After that, my warrior angels threw ropes on the bat-creature and took it to a different dimension. There were also snakes on my mountain. I commanded fire to come to burn them all. Sunshine appeared after that and a bright light cleared off my personal mountain making it shiny and clean.

I then sat on my seat of authority, which was a regal, golden-brass, royal chair, ornate with sapphire and topaz, precious stones. Anointed oil from Heaven and fire dripped down from the royal seat. Behind my royal seat was my guardian angel; he has long, dark hair. His name is Roshefim Esh, which translates in the Hebrew language to, Blazing Fire. He gave me my scroll of destiny.

I went over to my finance mountain that was guarded by my warrior angels. I was wearing royal, priestly white garments full of bright, glittering colors. Evil spirits tried to sneak in, but I cut their heads off and killed them all. The cave here was full of radiant diamonds. It was a magnificent slice of my journey with God.

Purified by Fire- Seraphim Angel

I went to the throne and saw myself in the river of life-fire where Jesus told me to soak my hands and body until I get purified, so the Seraphim angel took a ladle and poured liquid fire on my back. I looked closely at the angel who was very tall with a fiery-bright body with six wings.

Father's Chambers

I went in the spirit to a party in Heaven. Father, Jesus, Al, Glory angels and men in white linen were sitting at a long table eating, drinking, and fellowshipping. Jesus was sitting at the end of the table.

Jesus and I went on the dance floor. I was wearing a white dress and a crown of flowers on my head. I said Lord, "I would like to see Father face to face." On the right side of the crowd, a young man who had a short black beard came up to me. I hugged Him and looked closely to see His face. His face was soft like milk.

Father's eyes were very deep I could see the whole universe in them. My whole being became filled with intense happiness and joy.

I went with Him to His chambers to sit by a cozy fireplace. Al was here and he and I were facing Jesus and Father sitting on a couch. Angels arrived and served us cinnamon cookies and tea.

From here I went to my heart garden as a little girl dressed in a white dress with flowers. Jesus laid down in a field watching me as I was chasing butterflies.

Then we got transported to a waterfall. Jesus said this waterfall is special. You can walk through it and you won't get wet. We walked on the water through the waterfall to the other side to a cave. There was an angel that was lighting our path. We arrived at a wall where Jesus dug into it until He found an emerald, and put it in a sack. He took out more items: scrolls, crowns and precious stones, and a huge bright, light, green jewel. I also saw sacks full of diamonds in the corner of the cave.

We went back to the Father's chambers to show Him what was inside the sack. Father took two crowns and put it on our heads. The emerald was put on a pedestal.

We went to my finance mountain and gave the emerald, that had to be purified, to an angel. We later went back to the cave where Jesus took out a sapphire, an emerald and an onyx. He planted them in my heart garden. Out of the sapphire grew an intense blue stone.

The magnificent and holy Sapphire, in all its celestial hues, is a stone of wisdom and royalty, of prophecy and Divine favor. Sapphire of heavenly blue signifies the height of celestial hope and faith, and brings protection, good wealth and spiritual insight.

Spiritual Warfare by a Waterfall

I went in the spirit where Jesus and I were standing on a rock by our magnificent waterfall. We both dived into the water. We splashed and played in the water for a while and got out and climbed high up on the rocks. We both became white eagles with a wing span of more than eight feet and feathers whiter than snow. We flew above the waterfalls. The view from the top, overlooking the falls, was breathtaking. The falls were multi-cascading which roared down in many parallel chutes.

We flew up high, got into a steep dive, flew back up high again and dove down again in the water before we landed on the ground and became us again. In the distance about five miles away there was a hydra with seven heads. I saw many warrior angels surrounding the beast. These angels are the knights and commanders of the Heavenly host. They looked like well-built, muscle-men wearing ancient roman-type armor, wielding spears and flaming blazing swords. Al came also flying over with Whitey (his horse) and cut off the main head of the hydra. I went up on the cliff and blew up another head's beast another with my rocket-type weapon. Then the angels chopped off the rest of the hydra's heads.

While we did this warfare and defeated this beast there was no water in the bay. At the end of the battle we went to plunder. There were many big rocks with gold around it and numerous red rubies.

We put them in a sack and took them to my finance mountain. After we finished everything the water filled the valley and the sun came out.

I took some of the rubies to the sea of glass and I exchanged them for many scrolls. I went to the Court of Scribes to record the scrolls and put them in slots.

Al took a red scroll to the Court of Chancellors who stamped it, and then he went to the Court of Seventy.Here he received a mandate scroll that was written: "Africa".

We went to the throne room and we both bowed before God the Father casting down our crowns. Then Father gave us new glorious crowns. The crowns were ornate with emerald green and jasper. We went to the Father's chambers sitting by the fireplace, fellowshipping with Jesus and angels. They brought us cookies and tea.

How magnificent is to be in the presence of God.

Killing a Dragon - June 8, 2011

Al and I were standing in front of a strange looking dinosaur dragon that has a tail like a mace. I pointed my silvery sword at this creature. Lighting and fire came out of the sword, but the fire didn't affect it. The dragon opened its mouth and threw fire at us. We lifted our shields to protect us from the fire. Al pointed a sword at the dragon; thunder and electricity came out of the sword, electrocuting the dragon and it fell dead. Both of us cut off its head. We cut open its belly and took out a red vase with gold trim. Al took a scroll out of the vase and ate it. I took out a big ruby and I went to the sea of glass to exchange it for fifty red scrolls. I took them to the Court of the Upright and presented them as mandates that will be fulfilled later.

Jerusalem's Gates - June 2013

I went in the spirit where I saw myself as a small girl in a white satin dress. Jesus put a crown of white flowers on my head. He also gave me a white rose and told me to be pure as this white rose.

Al and I were ready for battle, wearing full metal amour. Jesus gave me a scroll and showed us a map of Israel.

We mounted our horses and went to Jerusalem. Big gates opened in front of us. We galloped through the streets until we arrived in front of a building; Al pulled out the map and read it with his warrior angels. After that the angels opened two big doors where a huge army was waiting for us. We went up on a mountain and were shown a valley and were told, "This is where the battle will take place."

Jesus gave us golden crowns and we sat on our seat of authority. He said, "You are kings in My kingdom, rule and judge righteously."

Defeating a Hydra with Seven Heads

I saw a hydra dragon flying around. It was throwing fire at us. Al flew with Whitey his horse towards the hydra and with one strike cut its head off.

Warrior angels shot many arrows at the hydra and blinded it. I was riding my horse Isaiah and bashed one of the heads with a mace. Some angels cut the rest of the beast's heads off. We finally defeated the beast, after a long battle.

Ecstasy in Indonesia

Jesus and I traveled to a very high mountain that was part of a mountain chain in Indonesia.

I said, "Jesus, what are we going to do here?"

Jesus replied, "Christians are persecuted here."

We traveled to a village that was recently attacked and was burning. Smoke and ashes were everywhere. Above the village we saw warrior angels surrounding a big cloud. Water from the cloud dropped down like a cascade and the fire was doused.

Jesus said, "This village was attacked by Muslims."

We approached a house that was in ruins. We carried a dead man out on a stretcher; his arms and face were badly burned. I took my emerald green jar out and poured oil over his wounds. His skin changed from black to red to yellow to normal color. I spoke life over this man, rebuked the spirit of death and he rose up from the dead. In amazement he looked at us puzzled, and then in an instant he recognized Jesus.

We went to another house where there was a dead child, mother and father. We took them all out on a stretcher. I rebuked the spirit of death and the girl rose up. Jesus just touched the parents and they also rose from the dead.

Praise God for the victory!

New Crowns and Armageddon

Jesus transported Al and I to a large room in Heaven that was full of treasures. Gold was everywhere, boxes full of treasures, sparkling. I found a golden sword.

I said, "Look Lord."

He said, "Take it."

I took the sword and put it in a scabbard. Jesus opened a box and gave us two keys, lots of scrolls, crowns and vials of oil.

He said, "Let's go to the throne and see Father."

When Al and I stood in front of Father, He put the new crowns on our heads and gave us new robes, mantles and staffs. Then we were given specific tasks for the end times. We were transported in the future where I watched the battle of Armageddon, that Al and I were part of. Jesus told us that we will defeat the last beast with the help of many warrior angles.

Al Killing a Dragon - November 1, 2009

Al and I were kneeling in front of Jesus as He anointed our heads with oil and gave us to drink a liquid that resemble honey.

Al's testimony is as follows, "I was wearing full armor on like a knight. I had my helmet on, breast plate, I was holding a spear in my hand, and I was riding Whitey. My horse was wearing heavy steel armor. I saw a tunnel in front of me and inside the tunnel were evil spirits. I pointed out my spear at them and made a way through them to the other side of the tunnel. When I got out I was above the earth.

After that we both saw this large dragon flying above us. With one strike I cut its head off. I went on the other side of the beast and sliced through its side. The angels came with a huge bag and took the remains away."

Three Doors in the Spirit

I went in the spirit with Jesus to a beautiful beach where there were two massive rocks by the ocean.

Jesus said, "Come."

Al also came and joined us. He had his armor on. Jesus found a spot on the beach and said, "This is the place." He put a white blanket down, laid a map on it and then showed us the places where we needed to go.

Jesus gave me a little bottle that had a long red neck and also three keys.

He also gave Al some scrolls. Jesus said, "Follow the map precisely." Al and I mounted our horses, followed by five angels. There were three doors that we had to walk through.

1st Door

I took a key and opened the first door. Inside there was an old-fashioned fireplace and a woman laying on a recliner chair, who was full of sores. I took out my red bottle with the long neck and applied this liquid all over her body. The sores disappeared. A number of cobras appeared in the room. I took my sword out and chopped their heads off.

The angels who were with us, cut the head off of a python that was approaching from behind. This went on for a while. There was also smoke in the room. I asked the Lord what was all of this. He said, "A witch lives here." I forgot to mention that I pushed this witch against the wall and wrestled with her before her healing.

She said, "Who are you? What is this power that you have? I lost my powers."

I replied, "We are messengers from God the Father and Jesus Christ the only Son, the One you should only worship. Your power is taken away because it's the power of the devil and he shall never prevail. Repent now and be changed in Jesus' name."

When the witch was healed, she was back on the recliner again, totally changed. Her face didn't look like an old, rugged, wrinkled woman anymore. Instead she was a beautiful, elderly woman with long gray hair. I poured healing oil from my emerald green jar over her body to complete her transformation.

When I was done, angels and I went out and turned towards the second door.

2nd Door

Using the next key, I opened the second door and saw a village called Chegilet in Kenya. There were huts all over the place. I released the angels into the huts to get the people out and follow us. Jesus told me to take everyone to this grassy area to preach the gospel of salvation to them. A healing angel poured oil over a crippled woman and she was healed. Then I asked, "Who wants to receive Jesus?" All of them put their hands up and received Jesus as their Savior.

3rd Door

I was then back in the spirit on the same beach with Jesus.

He said, "The third door one is more intense. Take the five angels with you."

I was traveling in a chariot with four horses. We rode for a long time. The chariot was covered and had two windows. There were fiery darts coming at us from all directions, but it ricocheted back.

The third door was over a cave that I entered followed by angels. There was a beast hiding in this cave. As we began to walk the beast approached us; it had a weird looking head, with the body of a bear. It swiped its paw at me but missed. I had a whip and a rope on my sides. I used the whip to lash at it. I quickly used the rope to tie it up around its neck, arms and legs. The angels carried the beast out.

Next in the cave, there were many big spiders coming at us. An angel lifted me up in his arms, as the spiders were crawling everywhere. Another angel used some kind of smoke to kill them.

The second beast looked like a prehistoric, saber-tooth tiger. I took some powder from a pouch on my side and blew it in its face killing it instantly. The angels dragged it out. After that a goat appeared with big horns and I threw some small spears into its eyes. The blinded goat was taken away by the angels.

I walked though the cave and reached a room that was full of treasures, but there was a barrier to go into the room. In the middle of the room, sitting on a rock, was a sparkling emerald vase that had a very bright, long neck. The Lord told me, that I needed to ask the angels to cover me as I go through this vibrating space. The angels covered me as we all stepped into the room.

I took the vase, turned around, and we all walked back to the cave entrance. We all took a chariot and traveled in the Spirit to the sea of glass.

"And I saw something like a sea of glass mingled with fire, and those who have the victory over the beast, over his image and over his mark and over the number of his name, standing on the sea of glass, having harps of God." Revelation 15:2

I exchanged the emerald vase for a box and three cubes on a string.

I took these items back to Jesus, where He was waiting for me on the beach. Jesus opened the box and there was a large sparkling-white diamond in it. He gave it to Al and I and said, "This is your treasure, as you enter the Promised Land."

Thank You Lord for all that You have shared with us to do in Your Kingdom.

All glory belongs to Jesus Christ and God the Father!

Killing a gigantic White Beast

I went to where Jesus was already waiting for me on the bench in my garden. He showed me a beautiful white rose. He said, "Be pure as this white rose." After that I saw beautiful doves flying with white ribbons in their beaks. The ecstasy shifted to a river where we walked barefoot through it. Jesus caught a fish, cooked it and we ate it under a tree. Around us was a beautiful meadow with magnificent purple flowers.

I asked the Lord, "Where is Al?"

Jesus pointed to where Al was. Al, in armor, joined us for a picnic. After we ate Jesus said, "I have great plans for both of you. You shall lack nothing. I AM! You are going to go to every nation and bring this revelation of Xtreme Big Game Hunting, spiritual warfare. I will send you to specific nations."

Both of us were on our horses in front of a gigantic, white beast. We cut off the beast's head with our swords, but its tail was still battling us. With a single strike Al cut off its tail. Then both of us cut its body up into pieces. Angels came to take the remains away.

Ecstasy above Africa

Al and I were kneeling in front of Jesus when He said, "Pull your swords out." They were very shiny to look at. Jesus took a bottle and anointed our heads and kept pouring, pouring and pouring. He gave us more weapons and tools. We mounted our horses and went towards this platform. We climbed stairs with our horses reaching the 1st, 2nd and 3rd platforms on the top of a high mountain.

Jesus told us, "Look down in the valley. That is Africa. See that dark forest between the mountain and Africa? Those are evil spirits trying to stop you. Take these bowls full of fire and pour them down in the valley."

When we poured the bowls, a golden, red lava path formed reaching down to the forest. Jesus said, "Follow this golden path and stay on it and you will be protected from the evil spirits."

We rode down with our horses until we reached the forest. As long as we stayed on the golden path, we were safe. We could see many evil creatures flying around us trying to intimidate us. I took my flame-thrower weapon from the saddle and killed many of the evil creatures. We passed the forest and finally reached Africa to meet with several leaders. After that I saw Al preaching and teaching the Word of God. We also cast out demons and healed the sick.

Killing another Dragon

I went to my personal mountain where there were warrior angels with long hair and full armor. I was wearing my shiny, silvery amour and was holding a bright-light, silvery sword. A dragon was throwing fire at us. One of the big angels started to wrestle with the dragon. The angel shredded it to pieces. I cut open its belly with my sword and collected all the rubies. I took the rubies and planted them in my heart garden. Beautiful red trees grew up with multicolored trunks and branches.

Jesus and I then enjoyed eating fruit under a tree in my garden.

Spiritual Warfare above Israel

I went to my heart garden where Jesus was waiting for me on a bench. Jesus gave me a white flower to smell. Then an angel brought a scroll. Jesus and I went for a walk in this beautiful garden that had a fountain. Father was there with the twenty-four elders. We all sat at a big round table where the angels passed scrolls around. When the angel gave me a scroll, my whole body became shimmery. I was wearing a white crown with white diamonds on it. We were all talking about Israel.

When an army of Malachim angels on horses approached us, my garments changed to full-body armor. In an instant we were above Israel where there was a dragon spitting fire. The Malachim angels surrounded the beast, threw many ropes over it, and restrained it.

With one big swing I cut its head off. When I cut open its body, serpents and many small dragons came out. The Lord told me to speak and when I did, I commanded all to be destroyed. After that I saw angels taking them to other dimensions, closing the portal behind them. Praise God for Victory in Jesus name!

I was then walking with Jesus in a river where we were picking up emeralds. They were in a calcite-shell matrix and we had to chop them out in order for this precious stone to be pure. We also picked up rubies. We went to my garden and put them on the table in a basket. I went to the bridal chambers where the floor was marble and a thick mist appeared in the middle of it. Jesus was making me a new crown. He decorated the crown with rubies, diamonds, emeralds, topaz, sapphire and amethyst.

Meeting Banai Elohim, Archangel Michael

I went to the throne room of Father wearing my royal garments; a golden robe with light, bright lace; my shoes were a marble-like color; the scepter that I was holding was emerald-green with shades of purple and gold; my crown was ornate with amethyst, rubies, emeralds, purple stones, gold and jasper stones. Father God was sitting next to me Who was full of light that radiated all through my body.

I got up from my seat of authority and went to the dance floor. Yeshua was dressed in Victorian clothes. I was wearing an amazing, beautiful red velvet dress. We danced a waltz with other royal kings. Father came also and danced with us.

After dancing I went to the Father's chambers and drank some tea next to a fireplace on the left side of the room. I always love the presence of Jesus, Father and the Holy Spirit here. The door opened and Michael the Archangel came in.

He is the leader of the Sons of God, Banai-Elohim canopy of angels. He had long black hair and was wearing full body armor that was a dark-silver color. He was holding a flaming sword in his hand.

Michael unrolled a scroll all the way to where Al and I were sitting. We picked up part of the scroll and read it. Golden letters came out in waves and entered in to us. The scroll rolled by itself back into the hand of Michael. We understood from the scroll that we are joining in a battle with Michael the Archangel.

The ecstasy shifted immediately to the place where angels were battling a dragon with many heads. Michael cut one of its head's off. I threw my boomerang-bladed weapon at it, chopping another head off. Al flew with Whitey and chopped another head off with his sword. Michael took the body of the beast and smashed it against a rock. The body broke in two and we took out a six-foot, white-golden orb. I went to the sea of glass and exchanged the orb for a trunk full of treasures. Jesus and I took the trunk to my heart garden, opened it and inside was gold coins, a new golden jar of liquid and five scrolls.

I asked the Lord about the scrolls and He said to me, "Five scrolls are five doors that you need to walk through."

1st Door

I took the first scroll which opened the first door. I was walking on a road that was paved with cobblestones. Multicolored flowers were everywhere. I arrived in front of a house and stuck the scroll in the ground. Hundreds of beams of light came out of the scroll emanating heavenly frequency. Inside the house there were four kids sick with malaria. The frequency and sound from the scroll entered the house and all the kids were healed.

2nd Door

I took the second scroll, entered a door, to see a map of the world with Jesus pointing to Congo. I took the scroll to a village and stuck it in the ground. A red liquid came out of the scroll like blood and healed a colony of lepers. Wow, what an amazing Father and Jesus!

3rd Door

I took the third scroll through a door to a village in Romania. I put the scroll in the ground and a multitude of people gathered and surrounded the scroll. A funnel of angels formed from Heaven to earth and a multitude of angels came out and gave scrolls to all the people there. Richard Wurmbrand appeared and said to the people, "My dear ones don't lose heart. I went to Heaven to be with Father but you continue the legacy, be forerunners in God's Kingdom and finish the race of Jesus Christ." After that Richard got back into the funnel with angels and disappeared. WOW!

Richard Wurmbrand was tortured for Christ in Jilava prison in Romania, spending fourteen years in solitary confinement. Richard Wurmbrand (March 24, 1909 - February 17, 2001) was a Christian minister, author, educator and founder of the Voice of the Martyrs.

4th door

I took the fourth scroll and went through a door following Jesus on a road. He was wearing a white robe with a hood. I asked Him where we were going. He told me that we are back in time where Stephen was stoned. We arrived at the place by the wall where Stephen was about to be stoned, when a powerful bright-light came from Heaven and Stephen appeared in his glory. Jesus nudged me to give him the scroll which I did. After that Stephen disappeared.

5th door

I took the fifth scroll and entered a palace. I walked into an office and gave a man the scroll. The man was a government official in Pakistan. His wife was sick with cancer and bedridden in a hospital. At the same time, Jesus and I went in the hospital to heal this woman. I had a new golden jar that Jesus gave me and poured a yellowish-liquid over her head. The liquid spread down to where her liver was. I looked inside her body and saw the liquid enveloping the liver and destroying all the cancer.

Seeing back at the official's office, he read the scroll and said, "Is this some kind of joke?" On the scroll was written that his wife was healed.

I replied, "No sir, your wife is healed."

The phone rang and on the other end of the line I could hear, "Sir, your wife is healed. She has no more cancer." He was shocked and couldn't believe it. He took his coat and ran out the door to the hospital.

Praise God for all His miraculous healings.

Hunting with Angels - June 19, 2017

I was in the spirit by a lake with Jesus, He said, "Come." Jesus caught a fish, cooked it, and we sat to eat it together. There's nothing like a fish fry on the beach with the King of kings!

After we ate, Jesus said, "I have an assignment for you. Go take warrior angels to this mountain."

I traveled with six warrior angels in a chariot and arrived at a mountain range. I got off the chariot and went inside a cave. There was a big beast inside the cave, growling at me. As it came forward to attack me, one of the angels cut off its paw. The rest of the angels tied it up with ropes and took the beast out of the cave.

I walked further inside the cave and looked up and saw stalactites hanging from the ceiling, sparkling like diamonds. I took my sword, cut some of them off and put them in a container.

As we went further into the cave, we came across a large pile of gold nuggets that I put in sacks. I walked over to a wall that was covered with brilliant-white diamonds. I scraped some of them off and put them in a sack.

We traveled back to the sea of glass in a chariot of angels. I exchanged everything for a sack full of scrolls. I took the scrolls to my throne in Heaven. Jesus and I were sitting on our royal thrones as we distributed the scrolls to many saints.

Raising a dead man in Switzerland

Jesus and I traveled on a road with six warrior angels. Far away I could see the Alps in Switzerland. We made a right turn down a hill through the woods walking for a while until we arrived at an open space. We found a dead man lying on the ground that was wearing hunting clothes. I looked at Jesus and He knew what I was thinking and said, "Breath the Ruah Breath of God in him."

So, I spoke the breath of God Ruah and the life of Christ upon this man's body. The man suddenly stood up and looked at Jesus scared.

Jesus said to him, "Don't be afraid, we are all here to help you." Jesus gave him a scroll. The man hugged Jesus and went on his way.

The Healing Mountain

I went to my heart garden where Jesus and I were picking fruit and

putting them in a basket. We sat down and ate them under a tree. Angels poured thick oil over my hands.

I went to my healing mountain which was covered by dark clouds that had a dragon flying over it. Evil reptile creatures were also there walking around. My warrior angels surrounded the mountain as fire-like rockets and bombs were thrown down from Heaven at this dragon. The dragon fell into the valley, dead and I cut its head off. The reptiles from my mountain were destroyed by fire. I asked for the sun to show up and bright light to come to my mountain and flowers sprang up around the rivers and lakes. It was such beautiful scenery. I then sat on my seat of authority. I was wearing a golden-white garment and had my crown on.

I shifted into the Father's throne room. It was awesome. I saw four living creatures, smoke was all around: Lion, Ox, Man and Eagle.

I saw Al approaching the throne. We both knelt down casting our crowns. Father gave us new crowns. We both went to the Court of Kings. There we were given many mandates and scrolls. We were assigned to sit at a table and many kings came to us with many scrolls and we stamped their scrolls. Men in white linen were there also.

Smith Wigglesworth approached Al to talk to him and give him a scroll. Later on Al put this revelation scroll in The Way book that he wrote with God.

A Purple Crown

My body was full of light as I entered my garden. After dancing with Jesus and Father, I went to the throne room where the Seraphim surrounded it. I shifted to the sea of glass, received many scrolls and ate some of them on my way back to Father's chambers by the fireplace. I was wearing priestly, golden royal clothes and a purple crown.

Purple is a mixture of blue and red. Blue is sometimes associated with the law or commandments of God and red is associated with war, blood, and judgment. Purple is very important in the accessories in the ancient temples of Israel including the curtain of the tabernacle, the veil of the tabernacle, the ephod of the high priest, the girdle that the high priest wore, the breastplate of the high priest and even the hem of the priests robe. Purple is associated with royalty, the rich, mystery and piety. It was also worn by Roman magistrates.

The door opened and Al walked into Father's chambers. He was wearing full-armor holding a sword that had blood on it. Ancient warrior angels were there. Other angels served us a drink that tasted like honey. One angel took out a big book.

I asked, "Father what is this book?"

He said, "This is your destiny."

Father gave us medallions. We mounted our horses and rode by an ocean on a beach. In the distance there was a hydra dragon. The angels threw ropes to hold it down. I flew with Isaiah and chopped off the beast's heads with my golden sword. Al took his sword and struck it in the middle and its body exploded. The remains were scattered all over the beach.

Al picked up a scroll that was rolled out with golden trim and he put it inside his armor. He took it back to the Father's chambers and hung it on a hook by the fireplace. The scroll rolled out on the carpet. He came back to the beach and helped me plunder all the purple diamonds. The purple diamond was radiant with many multicolored facets. Angels collected them into sacks.

Al and I walked through a silvery gate guarded by warrior angels to exchange the purple diamonds for a sack of scrolls. Al received a new sword and a treasure trunk. We took them all to Father's chambers. Al asked Father about the scrolls and He said, "Take them to the record room."

Al went to the record room and gave the scroll to an angel and asked, "What are these scrolls?"

The angel replied, "These scrolls represent assignments for your life. They are recorded here in the record room." Angels put them all in specific slots.

Spiritual Warfare in Israel

I went to my garden that had a beautiful water fountain. I took some water in my hands and drank. The water was of gold and silver drops.

Jesus said, "Come." He took my hand to attend a feast in Heaven. Father, Al and angels were there and we all sat at a long table. I was wearing my royal golden clothes. We all enjoyed eating, drinking and sitting at the table with the King.

After that, Al and I were transported to the Court of War. The cloud of witnesses was there also, which included Elijah, Isaiah, Abraham and Moses. We received golden scrolls that were signed by the cloud of witnesses.

There was a huge principality that looked like a python with multiple heads, circling around above Israel. Al and his ancient Malachim warrior angels surrounded the beast. I was riding my horse Isaiah.

Uriel the captain angel took his sword and cut the snake in the middle. Dragons and beasts came out of its belly and the rest of the angels engaged them in battle.Fire and thunder, arrows and rockets were flying around; the battle was very intense with smoke. One dragon came at me, but with one strike I cut off its head. There were millions of angels fighting this beast. Finally, Uriel killed the big dragon with a blast of fire bombs. The battle was won. Praise God for the Victory!

Jesus, Al and I, the cloud of witnesses and angels went to a street in Jerusalem. The angels poured out a turquoise liquid that filled the streets. A huge crowd of people came and surrounded us.

Moses stood in front of the crowd and said, "Men of Israel wake up. Stop going after false gods, false doctrines and false beliefs. This is Jesus Christ whom you crucified two-thousand years ago. He is coming back for a spotless bride. Believe in Him, trust in Him, receive Him and worship Him. He is your Lord. Be not faithless but a faithful generation."

Jesus stood in front of the people and raised His hands up high and said, "My sons and daughters, come. I Am."

All the Jews fell at His feet worshiping Him. Yeshua blessed them all.

After this amazing ecstasy and winning the battle in the spiritual realm above Israel, I was sitting comfortably in our car next to the lake filled with the frequency of Heaven. I looked at my right foot to see oil from heaven all over my foot. Wow! What an amazing Father in heaven. To Him be all the glory.

Resurrection in Himalayan Mountains

I went to the dance floor dancing with Yeshua wearing my red velvet dress. Father came along and we danced spinning around and around until we became blended together.After that Yeshua and I went to the waterfall, my favorite place. We dived under the water came out at the surface, splashing each other.

We came out of the water and walked behind the waterfall into a cave. I could see the light at the end of the cave and when we came out, we had been transported to the Himalayan Mountains.

Ethnic people such as Gurkhas, Kiranti and Nepalese were walking around with carts. Erelim Angels accompanied us. We walked for a while on a road, arriving at a village where we saw many dead bodies. I asked Yeshua why these people had died. He said many died of diseases and many were killed for their faith. Two angels came from the Court of Angels, carrying two glowing scrolls. They stuck them in the ground; one at the end of the village and the other scroll at the other end. When they did that, the bodies rose from the dead one at a time, looking glorified in creative light. Yeshua told me to preach the gospel to them and I also gave them Bibles.

Later, there was a woman screaming from a leg wound. I poured oil from the emerald green jar and she was healed.

I entered a hut where a woman had malaria. I spoke out the breath of Ruah over her and she was instantly healed.

Traveling to Jerusalem back in TimeWe walked into the old, Jewish quarter of Jerusalem.

The walled Old City is one of the oldest continuously inhabited cities in the world, with the Jewish quarter situated to the southeast corner. In 1948, the Old City was occupied by Jordon and most of the ancient

buildings were destroyed. In 1967, however, when Israel took control of the Old City, the remains were excavated and buildings reconstructed.

We entered into a building through a big wooden door on the left. Yeshua and I stood in front of another door. I said, "Can we walk through it?" Before I finished my sentence in a moment we were in a room where an orthodox, Jewish man was reading from the Old Testament.

The scripture that he was reading was from *Isaiah 53: "Surely He has borne our grief (sicknesses, weaknesses, and distresses) and carried our sorrows and pains [of punishment], yet we [ignorantly] considered Him stricken, smitten, and afflicted by God [as if with leprosy].*

But He was wounded for our transgressions, He was bruised for our guilt and iniquities; the chastisement [needful to obtain] peace and well-being for us was upon Him, and with the stripes [that wounded] Him we are healed and made whole.

All we like sheep have gone astray, we have turned everyone to his own way; and the Lord has made to light upon Him the guilt and iniquity of us all.

He was oppressed, [yet when] He was afflicted, He was submissive and opened not His mouth; like a lamb that is led to the slaughter, and as a sheep before her shearers is dumb, so He opened not His mouth."

An angel appeared and asked the man, "Do you understand what you are reading?"

The man was startled, rubbed his eyes in unbelief and asked, "Who are you?"

The angel replied, "I am Raphael." The angel asked again, "Do you know who Isaiah is talking about?"

The man said that he was confused and he didn't know who Isaiah was talking about.

Yeshua showed Himself to the man and said, "I AM."

The man got scared and fell to the ground. He said with a trembling voice, "This is not possible, this is blasphemy."

Jesus said, "Jeremiah don't be afraid" and He took him back in time through history.

Yeshua showed the man how He walked these streets of Jerusalem, proclaiming God's kingdom, healing the sick, raising the dead, casting out demons and preaching the Gospel. Yeshua also showed him how He rebuked the Pharisees and whipped people, kicking them out for defiling the temple of the living God. After that he took him to the cross and showed him how He died for his sins and bled for him to be saved.

The man was at the bottom of the cross looking up as the blood of Yeshua was dripping on his head. They both then transported back to the man's house.

The man was completely undone, crying on the floor, "Lord, Adonai, indeed You are Yeshua Hamashiach. Depart from me. I am not worthy."

Jesus said, "I have forgiven you. Believe in Me, receive and follow Me. Go and tell people how much Father loves them and what He has done for you."

Raphael gave Jeremiah a scroll, new clothes, robes, a scepter and a crown.

PRAISE GOD FOR HIS NAME IS GLORIFIED FOREVER!

I went to the bridal chambers where Father gave me a new robe of transparent-light of blue lace and a crown of love.

When I was soaking in His presence, the Light of Father changed from white-light to intense sapphire-blue. We both went to the dance floor and danced until I went up stairs to meet with the Spirit of Wisdom on wisdom heights. She was wearing a bright-orange robe. She asked me to come in. The room was beautifully decorated with red couches and pillows. She gave me a liquid to drink from a golden bottle. I said I would like to have wisdom to make decisions in ministry, business, dealing with people, etc. She handed me a scroll and said, "Eat." When I ate, several dozen more scrolls appeared and I ate them all.

I went back downstairs to the Father's chambers to dwell in His presence. Jeremiah walked in with a burning scroll that I ate.

Jeremiah said, "Fire will come out of your mouth, burning people like wood when you speak. It will change them."

I then went dancing with Yeshua wearing my royal, golden-lace clothes and a golden crown. Yeshua was wearing red clothes and a red crown. The Seven Spirits of God were all around us. Al came along dressed like a decorated soldier with a navy-blue robe. Father came to give us a red scroll that when we unrolled it was written the secrets and mysteries of Yahweh.

Fighting an Octopus Creature over Israel

I went to the bridal chambers, got in a tub prepared by angels, where I soaked with many fragrances like frankincense. I received new robes of

red with golden trim. The Spirit of the Lord was upon me. He put a purple crown on my head. Jesus and I met a man in white linen before we went to the dance floor and danced.

I went to the Father's chambers and sat by the fireplace. Al was there also. A big door was opened and a crowd of angels walked in. We were summoned to go to the Court of Seventy where we were surrounded by a cloud of witnesses and men in white linen. We all received scrolls. I saw Paul and Peter approaching Al saying to him, "I give you my mantle." They put a mantle on Al's shoulders.

I was then wearing my full armor riding Isaiah with chariots of angels above Israel. There was an octopus-looking creature ready to attack us with its tentacles. Arrows and fire were thrown at this beast. I drew my sword, cut off some of the tentacles and threw an ax in its eye. One tentacle tried to grab my waist, but an angel cut it off.

I pointed my fiery sword at the beast and burned it to ashes. Its body fell to the ground in a desolate place.

Receiving Scrolls

I went to Heaven to a field full of lilac and yellow flowers. Jesus made me a crown of flowers, put it on my head and we sat under a big tree in the garden. After a while we went walking through the river in my garden and I picked up an emerald stone. We went to the bridal chambers where Jesus gave me a golden robe and a green crown. Green represents the spirit of counsel. I went to the throne room of Father and cast my crown before Him. After that I went to the sea of glass and exchanged the emerald stone for three scrolls that were gold, silver and purple. I went to the Father's chambers next to a fireplace and received another purple scroll.

I saw Al and I with chariots of angels facing a black dragon.

I received a new sword in my hand, that was rotating 360 degrees, that had a silvery handle. I saw special, warrior angels with thunder and lightning coming out of their swords. With one huge strike I cut off the dragon's head, but another head popped out in its place. The dragon was throwing fire at us. I chopped all the heads and the wings off the dragon. When its body fell, I cut its belly open with my sword and collected precious, purple stones from it, went to the sea of glass and exchanged them for three vials of red, purple and yellow and two daggers.

Spiritual Warfare in Nigeria

I went to the Father's throne room and saw wheels within wheels and fire around the throne room, smoke and the four faces of God: Eagle, Ox, Lion and Man. A river of fire was coming from the throne. Father's hair was white as wool. I saw a bright light.

I saw huge wings of cherubim and the sapphire floor. It was such an awesome atmosphere. I took communion there: the bread and the wine.

I went to my heart garden where there were five, fiery scrolls stuck into the ground burning unwanted seeds. An old tree was dug out and a sapphire tree was planted instead. After that Jesus and I went to walk through a river where we picked up precious stones: topaz, emeralds and rubies. We went under my favorite tree and started to make robes, crowns and scepters for saints.

Jesus and I traveled to Jerusalem to a fountain in a square where we drank some water. We went inside a house where three women became followers of Jesus. We brought them mantles, crowns, scepters and robes.

Jesus said to them as He put the crowns on their heads, "You are now royal priests in God's Kingdom. Take your position of authority. Learn to rule, learn wisdom, knowledge and understanding. The Seven Spirits are here to train you."

Jesus and I went to Nigeria to a village where muslims had killed hundreds of Christians.

I said, "Lord what are we going to do?"

He said, "We need to do warfare. We need to get rid of the spirit of death."

Many chariots of angels came in surrounding this place. Three dragons were flying around. With three strikes I killed all of them with my sword. Another dragon popped out and was throwing fire at us. I pointed my rocket-weapon at it and blew it into small pieces. I saw many angels pouring oil over the village.

Then I asked Jesus if we were going to raise these people from the dead.

Jesus said, "Like Ezekiel spoke over the valley of dead dried bones, speak life over these people."

I commanded the dead to rise and I spoke the breath of God the Father to come into each body. The entire village was resurrected. They all bowed down to Jesus calling Him Yeshiva Hamashiach. The angels closed the portal of death over this village. Giant guardian and warrior angels were put over these places.

I went to the bridal chambers where Jesus gave me a multicolored, rainbow robe; the colors of the seven Spirits of God. I went to the Court of War where new scrolls were being signed and new strategies being assigned. Praise God for Victory!

Traveling to Cairo

Jesus and I traveled to Cairo. We walked on a cobblestone road by a grocery market. We crossed the street and entered a rugged old house with an arch-shaped entrance. As we entered, there was a sick man sitting on a bed. I had a doctor's bag with me. I opened it and took out a small bottle that had liquid of a golden-topaz color. I gave the bottle to Jesus. He gave it to this man to drink which made him throw up making him completely healed.

Another Octopus and Scrolls

Al and I went to a beach where we received an assignment to battle with an octopus looking creature with multiple tentacles. It was far in the distance suspended in the air. I took my sword and with one strike I cut it in two parts and it fell to the ground. I cut open the belly of the beast and took out a huge red ruby. I took the ruby to the Father's chambers where two angels walked in and brought three beautiful red velvet scrolls. One scroll had wooden tips on both ends with black writing on it. The second scroll had golden tips on both ends written with golden-fire letters on it. The letters lifted off the scroll and came into me. The third one had silver tips on both ends with white-light letters. Father told me to take the scrolls to the Court of Scribes to record them. After that I then took them to the Court of Chancellors before finally taking them to my finance mountain. Praise God.

Meeting Elijah

I was wearing a light-blue sparking dress and white crown as I danced with Jesus and Father.

He said, "You are my precious purple flower in the garden. You shall go far with Me. Don't get entangled with unnecessary stuff. Stay focused on the task that I give you."

I went to the Father's chambers by the fireplace where Al was sitting on the couch. Jesus was sitting opposite him. Special, elite force angels, together with men in white linen were also here.

Elijah was present and gave Al a scroll. Jeremiah gave me a silvery sparkling scroll. We were then taken to Israel to see three dragons and a hydra beast flying around over the land. Fire from above was targeting them. One of them started to throw fire at us. I held my shield up to protect myself and directed the fire towards the dragon and burned its face. The dragon turned away from me. After that I saw Al cutting the dragon with one strike from top to bottom. The beast fell down into a valley. I was riding my horse Jordan this time. Before this battle I went to the weapon room and took a long, bright-golden sword.

This sword transitioned from a short to a long sword. I pointed my sword at the dragon and it exploded. After that many little dragons appeared on the ground. I killed one of them with my ax. I cut open the dragon's belly and many rubies came out. Angels put them in sacks. I took the rubies to the sea of glass and exchanged them for a hundred scrolls.

My health may fail, and my spirit may grow weak, but God remains the strength of my heart. He is mine forever.

Defeating Four Witches

Jesus and I were looking over a waterfall that had about a five-hundred-foot drop when we became white eagles doing acrobatics in the air, diving down with high speed. Father was there flying with us too. When we reached the bottom of the waterfall, we became us again and dived in the water. Jesus swam deep down, grabbed a small trunk out and put it on a rock. When He opened it, He took out an ancient map, a scroll, a dagger and a compass.

Jesus said, "Follow Me."

We started our journey on a path in a forest accompanied by our warrior angels. Jesus was dressed different this time. He had leather armor on and was holding a sword. All of us were wearing armor and holding swords. We came out of the forest and followed the path next to a mountain on the right side and on the left side was a waterfall cascading into a river. We arrived at a wooden suspension bridge connecting one side to the other. We crossed over to the other side, arriving at an open field to see an unusual looking house in the distance. Smoke was coming out of its chimney. The house was round with a straw roof.

Inside there were four witches chanting around a boiling pot. A light from Heaven was illuminating this house as we entered. The witches couldn't see us yet. The light from Heaven exploded the huge pot, blasting the whole place. The witches had been chanting and cursing Christians all over the world.

After the blast, all of them lost their powers and were screaming, "What is happening? What is happening? All of our powers are gone."

Angels took them all out in chains and made them kneel down before Jesus.

Jesus pointed His sword at the witches and said, "Are you willing to repent and stop cursing my children?"

They said, "No."

Jesus ordered the angels to chop their heads off.

I said, "Lord, can I please ask, if any of them have any sickness in their body." Jesus agreed. I asked them the question. One witch said she had a hernia that was excruciating and painful. I asked her if it was ok to pray for her. She said yes.

One of the other witches shouted, "Olivia, don't do this, please."

The other replied, "Shut up Lorraine, I've been having this for way too long."

I said to Olivia, "Let's make a deal. I'll pray for you and if you get healed you receive Jesus as your Lord, and give up witchcraft."

She hesitated and said, "Oh... ok."

So, I placed my hand where her pain was, I rebuked the pain and commanded the hernia to dissipate. Frogs and small snakes came out of her mouth, together with a bunch of vomit. She was completely healed. She received Jesus and threw her clothes off and witchcraft tools and burned them all. Angels brought her a new white garment and a crown. Jesus placed a robe on her shoulders and put a crown on her head.

He said, "Welcome daughter in My Father's Kingdom."

Wow! What an amazing God.

After that Jesus turned towards Loraine and said, "Because of you, a portal of death was opened over my children. Do you repent?"

The witch said, "Never."

Jesus told the Erelim angels, "Take her away to a prison where she will be judged accordingly."

Jesus pointed the sword to the next one and said, "You have brought plagues against my children. Do you repent?"

The witch said, "No." Jesus said to the angel, "Take her away."

Jesus asked the last witch, "You have brought poverty and stole finances and success from my children. Do you repent?" She also said no. Jesus commanded the last witch to be taken away in chains. A chariot with angels and horses came and pushed all of them inside and took them away. When they arrived at the destination they were locked up in a spiritual prison with other demons.

The Light in Heaven exploded the witch house and the angels closed the demonic, occult portal above it. Angels came and poured oil to sanctify the land.

Praise God for victory belongs to Him!

Lion's Heart Medallion

I went to my heart garden where Jesus put a medallion around my neck that said: "Lion's heart"

I was walking behind Jesus in a river where He picked up a carbuncle, blue-stone and put it on the river bank. He picked up another huge precious golden-stone and chopped it up into many pieces.

Jesus reached down in the water and picked up a trunk. Other angels came to help. They put the trunk under a tree.
Jesus opened it and inside were lots of ancient weapons: swords, mace, gauntlets, and many scrolls. My Malachim, warrior angels came and took out a bow and arrows. I got a new sword that was shooting electricity and made a huge noise that shook the earth when I hit the ground with it. Jesus gave each of us a scroll. One scroll was a map of the Western Sahara and Morocco.

My horse Isaiah came and we all traveled to another dimension. We arrived at this portal where a hydra-beast-snake was. I used my new sword and electrocuted one of the hydra's heads. An angel with his sword on the other side of the dragon held his sword up and electricity came out and joined with the electricity from my sword. This burned the main hydra's head. Al was there also battling this beast. He cut off another head. Then all the angels put chains around this beast and took it to another dimension.

There was another dragon flying around and the razor-blade angel killed it by shredded it to pieces. After this beast was conquered another huge python-beast came out of a hole that was killed. This evil portal was closed in the spirit and the hole was closed in the ground. Then the ocean covered the entire place.

Emeralds and Rubies

I went to the Father's chambers and gazed at the fireplace. I put my hand through the flames but it didn't burn me. I sat on the couch next to Al, facing Father and Yeshua on the other side. Angels brought us lemon and cinnamon cookies. The awe and atmosphere of Yahweh's presence was truly indescribable.

A door opened and Bob Jones walked in followed by his angels. Al followed him together with a warrior angel and went out the door to another room.An angel approached me caring many vessels on a tray. Lynn Collins, Al's mom, walked in and prayed for my hands and feet as I had been battling with skin issues for years. Jesus told me that healing will be progressive.

Al came back with a big trunk of goodies. When he opened the trunk, he took out a bronze spyglass, an ancient map and a giant book. He put the book on a pedestal and started to read it. After that I went to the library with Bob Jones and he placed a red stamp on my forehead and said, "You are sealed with the Father's love, power, justice and mercy. You are an overcomer. The Blood of Yeshua covers you. Nobody will come against you and even if they try, they shall become dust in the wind. Focus on Yeshua, write your book. It will be very successful."

Al and I went to the throne room and bowed down before Father and cast our crowns. Yahweh came over, picked them up and put them back on our heads. Father gave Al a new sword that vibrated and changed colors from gold to red to silver. I went to the weapon room and got a mace and a harpoon. The harpoon was so big my angels had to carry it out. I was thinking, "I wonder what this can do?" So, I pressed the button and the harpoon shot a ten-foot spear out that had a chain attached to it.

All of us went out and got into a big chariot that was pulled by twenty horses and accompanied by hundreds of angels. We arrived above an ocean and when I looked bellow, a thick mist was surrounding the entire place. A beast with a snake head came out of the water raging at us. I shot my harpoon, impaling the head of the beast through the skull. The beast was defeated. The body was carried onto a beach by the angels.

Al flew with Whitey and struck the head of a black dragon with his new sword.

Another beast with three heads came out of the water and I shot the harpoon again aiming for its body. The spear went through the beast and chained up the whole body. This beast was carried onto the beach also.

We then went to plunder. When I cut open the belly of the first beast, rubies the size of rocks came out. The second beast had green emeralds in it. Thousands of emeralds and rubies were lying on the beach. Angels gathered them into big sacks. I asked Yeshua what shall I do with all the rubies and emeralds and He told me to take some to my finance mountain, some to the prayer mountain and some to the sea of glass. Together with the angels we took sacks of rubies and emeralds to my finance mountain. I took some rubies and emeralds to the sea of glass and I exchanged them for three sapphire scrolls and two golden scrolls.

I took the sapphire scrolls to the Chancellor Court. I also took them to be recorded at the Court of Scribes.

After that I kept a big ruby and a big emerald stone in a backpack and Yeshua and I got translated to the Amazon in South America. We found ourselves in the middle of a tribe that were chanting. The witchcraft was very heavy. Jesus told me to take the ruby out and to stick it in the ground. The moment I stuck the ruby in the ground the whole place exploded, more specifically, all the witchcraft chanting tools. Five weird looking men freaked out and looked at me very angrily. Yeshua made Himself visible to them and when they saw Him, they fell like dead at His feet and couldn't talk anymore. Jesus told me to preach the gospel to the men. I said that God the Father is the only true God and that their Heavenly Father loves them very much and He created everything around them. He sent His Son to die on the cross for them and paid with His blood to wash away their sins. One of the men had an eye missing. I blew Ruah in his eye and a new eye formed in his socket. They all received Yeshua as their Savior. We gave them Bibles and we went on our way to our next assignment.

After that Jesus and I journeyed to a village in Africa. I took the emerald green stone and stuck it in the ground in this village. All the people were healed from all the diseases such as malaria, dysentery and many other diseases.

Raising the Dead in the Spirit

I was traveling with Jesus through a forest arriving at a beach where two bodies had washed up on the shore. Jesus told me that there will be more bodies coming up. There were five bodies soon lying on the beach dead.

I said, "Lord what happened?"

Jesus replied, "They drowned."

"Are we going to raise them from the dead," I asked?

"Yes."

I took a vile out of my bag and poured it in one man's mouth. His body became translucent and I could see all the veins in his body looking like trees. We repeated the same process for all of them. Suddenly the bodies rose from the dead and stood up. They all lined up like soldiers. Jesus gave each of them a scroll. After that we all went to camp by a fireplace. I asked them where they were from.

And they replied, "Tunisia."

I said, "Wow, what happened to you all?"

"There was a storm, the boat flipped and we drowned."

I said, "Are you muslims?"

They said, "We use to be, now we are believers in Jesus."

Praise God. To Him be all the Glory.

A Diamond Tree in my Heart Garden

I went to my garden where Jesus was waiting for me under this gorgeous, sparkling, diamond tree. He gave me a big, yellowish fruit to eat, but I couldn't taste it.

I asked what about that multicolored angel that we met the other day at the restaurant?

He said, "He's here."

The angel came down and sat with us under the tree.

I said, "Lord, can we battle together in the spirit?"

Jesus said yes.

So, both of us went to the weapon room where an angel pointed me to this strange looking weapon with 360-degree blades all around it, with an ax, a sword and with a mace on top.

We went into a strange, foggy place where an angel pointed at a dragon's head that came out of the fog. I threw this new special weapon at it and cut its head off and the weapon came back to my hand like a boomerang.I threw my weapon out again until all the heads were cut off and the dragon was killed. Al joined the battle also striking the dragon's body in two parts. After that I saw a group of angels closing this evil portal in this dimension.

Mighty Ones

I walked with Jesus by these amazing multi-cascading waterfalls. The waterfall was on the left and rocks on the right. Jesus was wearing beautiful white linen. I was wearing my silvery full armor. We transported to a forest where there were mighty ones called Erelim angels wearing full-body armor had us follow them. The angel's armor was amazing: their shields were metal that had flames coming out of it; their swords was blazing with golden fire that had silver handles; they were wearing metal shoes; breast plates made of iron, gold and silver meshed together, with leather straps on their shoulders. They were wearing red robes of fire. Jesus and I followed them through the forest arriving at the edge of a cliff over an escarpment. On the other side of the land there were many dragons, hydras and evil spirits. The Erelim angels began to shoot arrows with fire at them. *("But God will shoot them with his arrows; they will suddenly be struck down." Psalm 64:7)*

I flew with Isaiah my horse and chopped off three heads of the dragon. One hunter angel, also called a razor-blade angel, shredded the beast to thousands of pieces.

Deep into the ravine which slopes very sharply down, a huge snake appeared. Malachim angels came and burned it with fire.

After this amazing victorious battle, the land united with a big loud noise. The Lord told me to speak life over the land and the vegetation began to grow.

Killing a beast with Sandelphon Angels

Jesus and I were walking in my garden. Father came and we all sat down on a bench by the river. There was a goldfish doing laps in the water. I was so amazed how beautiful it was. Angels came bringing small golden cups on a pillow. Jesus gave me to drink from one of the golden cups. It looked like a thick golden-liquid. Malachim angels, Moses, Paul, Peter and John come into my garden. They each had a scroll. Moses gave me a scroll to eat which tasted bitter sweet. Paul also gave me a scroll to eat that tasted like honey and butter. Father gave Al a scroll.

My horse Isaiah came nodding his head anxious for the battle. I missed Isaiah, as I caressed his mane.

A weird looking dragon with many heads appeared.

Warrior angels called Sandelphon Ischim surrounding this beast. One of the heads threw fire at me. One Ischim angel held his shield and deflected the fire at the beast. The fire burned its head and it moved away.

With one swing I cut off one of the dragon's heads. Al chopped off another head. Then the rest of the heads were cut off by angels. The center body of the beast had a brain that was programming this beast. One angel told me, that brain has to be destroyed. I flew with Isaiah, penetrated its brain with my sword and it exploded. Victory again in Jesus!

After that we all came back to my garden. Jesus congratulated us and put leis of purple flowers around our neck.

Al and I both knelt before Jesus and He said, "Blessed are you my great warriors."

Planting Pine Trees in my Heart Garden

I went to my heart garden where Jesus was under a tree waiting for me. We went for a walk where He showed me a row of weeds that needed to be pulled out. We began to pull out shrubs and weeds out from the roots. A healing angel came and poured oil into the holes. We then planted different trees of pine, juniper, acacia, and orange. We also planted many flowers such as pansies, lemongrass, purple flowers, white roses and calla lilies.

I scanned around the garden and spotted something hiding in the trees. I sent Erelim angels to kill an animal that looked like a buffalo and I chopped a snake with my sword. There was also another small snake that was destroyed with fire. My garden was cleaned.

Adventure with my King in Tel Aviv

I met Jesus under a tree and He said, "I've been waiting for you."

He was wearing a white robe with a strapped bag over His shoulder. I sat next to Him and leaned on His shoulder. He kissed my forehead.

He said, "Come we have work to do."

So, we walked down this hill through a small forest to a city. We passed through the same square where we'd done many healings before. We walked by tall buildings, crossed the street and went inside an apartment building.

I asked the Lord, "Where are we?"

He said, "Tel Aviv."

On the other side of this building was the Mediterranean Sea. We went inside an apartment where a group of concerned orthodox Jews were talking to each other. They couldn't see us. Jesus and I went to a room in the back where an elderly lady was lying in bed.

Jesus put His hand on her forehead. She had a really bad fever. Jesus asked me, "You still have the emerald oil jar, right?"

I said, "Yes Lord."

"Let her drink from it," Jesus said.

I gave her to drink and her eyes opened gazing around. She could see me, but she couldn't talk because her pain was intense.

She also had gangrene on her left foot. I asked, "Lord how do you want me to pray for her?"

He replied, "Rebuke the fever," which I did and the fever left. Jesus rebuked the pain in her foot and her foot became normal. After that she looked at Jesus and He smiled at her. She stood up totally healed and amazed at this miracle.

She walked out of the living room and one of the men standing around said, "Mom you should be in bed what are you doing up?"

She said, "I'm fine. Jesus healed me and yes, He is Yeshua Hamashiach (which is the proper title in Hebrew for Jesus Christ)." She sat down in a big chair and they gave her something to eat. People were marvelling and also grumbling among themselves. Now they could see me but couldn't see Jesus yet.

The elderly lady said, "Jesus is Lord. He is alive. Listen to what she has to say."

I said, "Yeshua Hamashiach, He is the Messiah. Two-thousand years ago, He walked these very streets of Israel, did miracles, healed people, raised the dead, and you've rejected Him, crucified Him, but He rose to life, follow Him."

One of the orthodox Jews said, "This is blasphemy."

I said, "Look, your mother is healed, you still don't believe? Let's make a deal. Bring me someone here who is sick and if the Lord heals the person then you will accept Him and acknowledge Him as Yeshua Hamashiach."

A man on crutches walked over to me. His leg was in pain. I took my emerald green jar and poured oil over his foot. Jesus was watching me. I rebuked the pain commanded all the ligaments and bones to come into alignment with God's will. When his foot went from flexion to extension, he pushed the crutches away and started walking. He was astonished. All the orthodox Jews marveled at this miracle.

Then Jesus, materialized in front of them and all of them fell like dead at His feet calling Him, "Adonai, Yeshua Hamashiach."

Yes, indeed the power of Jesus is limitless. We can do even greater things than He did. He will slay satan with His breath.

Traveling to India

Jesus and I went to India to rescue some Christians that were locked in a prison. We gave them some robes and translocated them out to another place. I lookedabove India in the spirit and saw a principality that wanted to eradicate all Christians and make the country all hindu. I saw a dark creature sitting on the throne. I wanted to strike it with my sword but Jesus said, "Not yet."

I asked Him if we can at least restrain him and He said yes. Warrior angels came and brought a big, circle ring of chains and put them around the beast.

I went inside a hut where a man was laying dead on the floor and I raised him.

At another house a woman was crying because her husband was dead. Jesus told me to lay hands on him and I commanded the spirit of death to come out and it did.

163

The man stood up astonished. The woman was crying for joy.

Jesus and I went to a beach where there was a man without a leg. I saw in the spirit a new leg in the body parts room of Heaven. I took the leg and put it into this man. Praise God another miracle.

Purified with Fire

All of us were back in the Father's chambers fellowshipping by the fireplace. Angels were giving us cookies. It was awesome. Father gave each of us a box. Al opened his gift box that had lots of scrolls, a dagger with a silver handle, a sword and a bow with arrows. He also found a chain with a locket at the end that Jesus put around his neck.

I opened my box which had a necklace with a light-green gem. Angels took us to the corner of the room where there was a huge bathtub. It was like the flesh from our bodies got opened up like a zipper. We both sat in this tub and angels purified us with oil and fire. They gave us new robes and priestly garments, put crowns on our heads, scepters in our hands and we sat on our mountain of authority.

Father said, "You've been purified and washed clean, stay on the narrow path. You are rulers in my Kingdom. You've been given a galaxy to rule. Guard your heart and your mind. Trust Me, I Am."

The Mystery of God's Kingdom

I saw the hand of Jesus reaching out to me. We were surrounded by angels with beautiful garments. Jesus crowned me with a crown of flowers. I was wearing shiny, silvery-armor of a shield, sword, breast-plate and a white robe on my shoulders. I saw Al in shiny, silvery-armor also.

We were both in front of stairs where Jesus was waiting for us at the top. We both knelt and He gave each of us silver swords. He also put crowns on our heads and gave us both a key.

I asked the Lord, "What is this key?"

He said, "These are the keys that will unlock the mysteries of God's Kingdom."

"I will give you the keys (authority) of the kingdom of Heaven; and whatever you bind [forbid, declare to be improper and unlawful] on earth will have [already] been bound in Heaven, and whatever you lose [permit, declare lawful] on earth will have [already] been loosed in Heaven." Matthew 16:19

I went in the spirit to a mountain. There were lots of colorful flowers and I was playing in a field with Jesus. Jesus and I went to another part of the mountain where He put my armor on, "You are going to battle, take Isaiah with you."

I mounted Isaiah and an army of angels joined us. Jesus was leading the army. What a privilege to ride with my King of kings! I saw myself riding with chariots of angels.

There were thousands of chariots. When we came upon a dragon, all the angels shot their arrows at it. When Al on Whitey cut the dragon's head off, it fell dead in the valley.

Together with angels we went to plunder it. Out of the belly of the dragon came huge diamonds as big as rocks. The field was full of bright, sparkly, multicolored diamonds that we put in sacks.

I asked Jesus what we were to do with them. He said we were to take them to Al's finance mountain.

It was so amazing there with a cave of diamonds. The angels took the diamonds we'd collected and put them inside the wall. We walked inside a hallway, arriving at some doors that opened to reveal a wave of diamonds that filled up the room.

Gates of Jerusalem

During worship I saw many angels flying around holding many white ribbons forming like a gazebo around Jesus. Jesus was holding His arms out while angels were worshiping Him.

I saw a beautiful, long, iron-sculpted gate. I was gazing for a while at the gate and I asked Jesus what is this gate for Lord?

Jesus replied, "Those are the gates of Jerusalem."

The gates opened revealing an army of horsemen with full armor holding spears and swords entering the gates of Jerusalem. There were so many of them they filled the streets. They stopped at the bottom of white stairs. Jesus walked up the stairs wearing a bright-white robe with a purple sash. He reached His throne and sat down. There were two Seraphim angels at His left and right-side worshipping.

Every warrior bowed down with their horses before the Lord and they were quiet, eager to hear what the Lord had to say.

An angel had a scroll in his hand that he let roll all the way to the bottom of the stairs.

I picked it up and started reading the scroll, "These are the days of a new era where the Kingdom of God is being established; an era in which no evil will rule; an era in which the Kingdom of God is exalted; an era where all children are ruling from their mountain; an era where no man shall be in control but God is ruling; an era in which the Kingdom of God is exalted."

PRAISE GOD!

Another Journey to Israel

Jesus and I were swimming in the waterfall, splashing and having fun.

Jesus said, "Follow Me."

We went behind the waterfall into a cave. Jesus broke a wall with a stick allowing lots of emeralds and diamonds to fall to the floor. Angels put them in sacks and took them to my finance mountain.

Jesus and I were then in a boat at Eilat in Israel. We got out of the boat and went on a beach where there were five people dead. Jesus told me to speak Ruah breath on them and all of them rose up from the dead.

We went on a boardwalk walking by many shops. I saw a man on crutches. I approached the man and asked him if he would like his pain to go away and if I can pray for him. He said yes, so I rebuked the pain and commanded healing to come into his leg. He leaned his crutches against the wall and walked, totally healed. Praise the Lord! I said Jesus did this for you, trust Him. The man was speechless and astonished at this miracle.

After that Jesus and I went inside a building and found a woman that was on life support with many transfusions hooked up to her body. I asked Jesus what was wrong with her. He said that she has last stage cancer. I asked Jesus how we are going to heal her. Jesus looked intensely into her eyes and demons jumped out of her. My warrior angels took them away in chains.

I took oil from my emerald green jar and poured it all over her face and Jesus gave her to drink from this purple-yellowish liquid. The liquid that she drank went inside her body killing all the cancer cells. She got up looked at herself in the mirror and her whole countenance changed. She turned towards Jesus and fell at His feet crying for joy.

Jesus touched her head and said, "Blessings my daughter."

PRAISE GOD FOR THIS VICTORY!

Meeting the Cloud of Witnesses

"Therefore then, since we are surrounded by so great a cloud of witnesses [who have borne testimony to the Truth], let us strip off and throw aside every encumbrance (unnecessary weight) and that sin which so readily (deftly and cleverly) clings to and entangles us, and let us run with patient endurance and steady and active persistence the appointed course of the race that is set before us,

Looking away [from all that will distract] to Jesus, Who is the Leader and the Source of our faith [giving the first incentive for our belief] and is also its Finisher [bringing it to maturity and perfection]. He, for the joy [of obtaining the prize] that was set before Him, endured the cross, despising and ignoring the shame, and is now seated at the right hand of the throne of God .Hebrews 12: 1-2

The witnesses are in white linen who appear in various places around the world; the saints of old who have gone before us. They stand with us in agreement and they are there to encourage us. The cloud of witnesses is in the Court of the Upright and there you can present scrolls, mandates and blueprints for advice.

I went to my garden and I jumped in the middle a beautiful water fountain and splashed around. I took some water in my hands and it became drops of gold. I drank the water and splashed Jesus with it.

Jesus took my hand and we went to a big feast. We sat at a long table. I was wearing my long, golden, royal robe with a royal crown. Everyone was there: Father, Al, angels, Moses, Elijah, Isaiah, Abraham. Al and I received five golden scrolls and we went to the Court of Kings for them to be signed.

Father's Chambers

I went under my big tree in my garden. I hugged Jesus and He gave me grapes to eat. Father joined us. As soon as I saw Him, I cast my crown to the ground and I told Him how much I love Him.

We were surrounded by vibrant colors of blue, red and pink flowers as we walked to Father's chambers by the fireplace. Shining ones- angels- Chashmalim angels, who change colors, were surrounding the Father's chambers. These angels filled the room with multidimensional colors and music that came out of their bodies with high-pitched notes. Our bodies began to change into the same colors as the angel's. It was an indescribable experience.

Messenger angels brought a large platter of fruit for us to eat that we ate as we all fellowshipped together.

Body Parts from Heaven

I'm in the spirit and saw Jesus in front of me saying, "Come to Me." I see Him in a white robe putting a crown of flowers on my head.

I asked Him if Daddy Father can join us.

He replied, "He is walking on the beach." We both went and joined Father. It was so awesome.

Next, Jesus and I were walking on the streets of Jerusalem. I said to my Lord, "Can You teach me how to bring what is in the spiritual realm to the natural realm?"

Jesus pointed at a woman without an arm. Suddenly, I went in the body parts room in Heaven and saw an arm sitting on a self. I took the arm, brought it to this woman and put it into her. Her new arm was fully functional. She was perplexed when she saw what God did for her. She jumped and praised the Lord.

Next, we saw a man with crutches walking toward us, with no leg. I went back to the body parts room and found a leg on a self, brought it to the man, then he had a new leg.

Jesus and I went down some stairs in a prison made of old stone. Jesus had a bucket of water and started giving water to prisoners through metal bars. When He finished giving them water we appeared inside a man's cell. There was a man under a blanket that was full of wounds. Jesus touched him and all the wounds disappeared. Jesus and I went out of the cell; He gazed at the prison doors; raised both hands and all the doors exploded. All the prisoners got out.

After that we went walking through Jerusalem and in front of us there was a fountain. I drank some water from the fountain. A few feet from us there was a man sitting down begging who was missing a foot. Jesus approached him touched him and suddenly his foot grew out.

We went to a woman's house that had three children. One of the kids was sick with tuberculosis. I poured oil over his head and he was healed instantly. The mother fell at Jesus feet rejoicing, receiving Him as her Savior and was healed emotionally.

We got on a fishing boat with Jesus' disciples and pulled up a net of multitudes of fish that we fried up on the beach and ate.

Healing a Man without a Leg

We approached a man whose right leg was missing. I asked him how long he'd been like this.

He said, "I had an accident where heavy equipment fell on my leg."

In a flash Jesus told me in the spirit, "There is trauma in this man's emotions and also depression. So, you need to get rid of this evil spirit of trauma first." Jesus also told me to ask the man about depression.

I asked the man, "How long have you had depression?"

He said, "As long as I can remember."

I prayed in the spirit and asked my warrior angels to take the demons of trauma and depression out and put them into a spiritual prison. I saw angels put them in chains and take them out.

After that I commanded the leg to grow out and it did in an instant. I said to the man, "Get up and walk."

He stood and was so shocked he didn't know what to say. He shouted for joy hugging Jesus and I. I asked the man if he would like to receive Jesus as his personal Savior and he did.

Praise God!

The Silver Necklace

I went to my Father's chambers by a beautiful fireplace. Jesus and Al were there. Doors opened and a huge group of warrior angels with full armor on came in.They each had scrolls in their hands. Al received a scroll and started to read it. One angel sat down next to us enjoying our company. Jesus put a silvery necklace around my neck.

We went under a tree in my garden where He handed me an apple. He also gave me a beautiful emerald ring. We picked up a green gem from the ground; took it to my finance mountain where the jeweler-angels broke it into small pieces, shaping them into gems with many facets.

Warfare in Tanzania

I went to the Fathers throne room and sat next to Him. Jesus gave me a new golden crown with jewels on it of onyx, beryl and sapphire. We all went to the dance floor and danced together. It was magnificent.

Jesus and I traveled in the spirit to Tanzania where a group of Christians gathered. We had been praying for them. Jesus and I went inside a hut where a woman was lying on the floor. She wasn't breathing.

I put my hand on her chest and I commanded the life of Christ to come inside of her body. She opened her eyes and stood up and looked amazed. Praise God for this resurrection.

There was a team of people praying outside a house. A black dragon was flying above us throwing fire at us. We both held our shields up to protect ourselves from the fire. A Christian warrior and I mounted our horses and we went to battle this dragon. With one strike he cut off its tail.

We were also surrounded by Malachim, warrior angels.

They started to throw missiles at the dragon. With one high jump in the air I flew with Isaiah my horse and chopped the dragon's head off. Prior to this Jesus gave me a new sword that had a handle decorated with sparkling jewelry. There was a huge snake taunting us from the distance. I threw my new sword up in the air and it twirled like a helicopter, chopping the snake into small pieces.

Angels came to pour a green liquid on the ground filling up the entire region. I asked the Lord what was this shimmery, green-smoky liquid. He said it was to keep the witches and witchcraft away.

Healing in Tanzania

I went back to Tanzania with my angels where the team were working. We walked on a path as we followed Jesus. In the distance was a large crowd that surrounded three dead people: two women and a man. I got close to the bodies lying on the ground and laid my hands on them and said, "Get up in the name of Jesus." All three of them rose from the dead. One woman was coughing up snakes. I saw Brian cutting the snakes head off with his sword. One of the men got up and walked. Praise God for resurrections. The other one followed also.

Out in a tall field of bushes, was a beast that was growling at us getting ready to attack, but a huge Erelim warrior angel, suspended in the air, shot arrows as fast as bullets can come out of a gun, destroying it. Angels then poured oil over the people.

Jesus and I continued our journey approaching a hut made of straw. Inside there was a blind woman cooking food.

Jesus said, "Take a few drops from your emerald green jar and put it over her eyes."

When I put some drops on her eye sockets Jesus said, "See how the eyes are forming into her sockets."

Two beautiful green eyes formed inside her sockets. The woman started to scream and shout when she saw Jesus. She was laughing and crying at the same time.

She said, "My God and My Lord, thanks to You I can see the Son of God."

We both hugged her and continued on our journey.

Yeshua and I Traveled in a Chariot

I was walking behind Jesus on a beautiful beach, watching Him as He made foot prints in the sand. We found a rock, sat on it, and gazed at the ocean. Jesus pointed at something in the distance that was coming towards us. It was a stunning chariot of angels. One of the angel's hair was long like bright-light, flipping in the wind.

When they reached us, Yeshua and I went for a ride in the chariot. We traveled over clouds, mountains, forests until we arrived at a big castle. Jesus was carrying a small case like a doctor's bag. The castle had dozens of rooms. We entered one room where an elderly lady was laying in bed sick from tuberculosis. Jesus took out a light-green vial from His case and gave her some to drink. I poured oil over her head from my emerald green jar. She started to cough several times, and after that she got up, walked around jumping for joy, praising God for her healing.

We continued on our journey where a chariot brought us to a jungle in the Amazon. A man was wounded with an arrow in his side lying on the grass. As Jesus carefully took the arrow out, I took a small dagger from my side that was already fiery, red-hot; seared his wound; poured oil over him while Jesus patched up the wound. The man got up, looked astonished at his side, and realized that he was healed, hugged Jesus and went on his way.

Diamond Tree

I went in the spirit by our gorgeous waterfall. Jesus and I dived in the water, splashed around and played in the water. When we got out, we went into my garden where I saw a sparkling diamond tree with multicolored fruit on it. We sat under the tree where He gave me a multicolored pear to eat. It had an unusual taste like honey.

Then I said, "Where is Father? I miss Him." When Daddy came, He gave me a scroll that I planted in my garden sprouting a beautiful, white, sequoia tree.

We walked to a blue river where there was a small castle on the top of a hill. Angels were picking up emeralds and putting them into a wall.

We went into the Father's chambers where angels brought us cinnamon cookies and tea to drink. After that we all went to the dance floor where all the saints were and danced. While I was dancing with the Father, I asked Him if He had a word for us for 2019. Father gave me a scroll and it was written in big letters: "BREAKTHROUGH!"

Journey with Jesus to Australia

I saw myself at Sydney harbor with Jesus traveling in a boat going under the bridge. It was beautiful. When we got off the boat, we entered a building where there was a man with two kids that were sick with a cold. I took some drops from my emerald green jar and put some in the kid's eyes, made them some tea and they got healed.

We then went to the opera house square where there was a man sitting on some stairs without a leg. In an instant I went to the body parts room in Heaven, picked up a leg sitting on a shelf and brought it back to the man.

He started to walk like he never had any problems. It was amazing.

Singapore Journey

Jesus and I traveled to Singapore. We walked through a huge crowd on the side of a street where we saw a man lying on the ground that had a knife in his chest. Jesus took the knife out and I poured oil over the wound. I rebuked the spirit of death and I spoke the life of Christ into his body. The man stood up and was astonished at this miracle.

Healing a Man on a Beach

I saw Jesus in the spirit sitting by a fire. He was playing with a stick in the sand.

Jesus said, "I've been waiting for you."

He was carrying a bag on His shoulder. In the distance we saw a mob of people stoning a man. We approached the crowd together with some Mighty Ones, warrior angels. The rocks they were holding in their hands levitated in the air and disappeared. The mob's eyes were opened in the spirit and as soon they saw the angels they got scared and ran away. Jesus and I approached the man that was lying in the sand. He had a broken arm and a huge bruise on his head. Jesus instantly healed his arm and I poured out oil from my emerald green jar over his head and the man got healed. He stood up amazed praising God.

Jesus asked him, "Why do these men stone you?"

The man answered, "Because of my faith in God. I use to be a muslim, but now I am a Christian." Jesus and I blessed this man and we continued our journey.

As we walked away from the beach we went towards a village. We walked through a big market full of people selling fruit and vegetables, live animals and all sorts of things.

I asked the Lord, "Where are we?"

He said, "Palestine."

177

We left the market and went down some narrow streets. We entered a house where inside there were five women wearing long, black clothes, mourning over another woman lying in bed. This woman had been beaten by her husband and she had bruises all over her face. Her husband beat her because he found out she was secretly a Christian. I poured oil all over her face and arms and she was instantly healed. Jesus made Himself visible to these women and they all fell at His feet. We gave her a Bible and she hid it under her long garments.

Journey with Jesus to India, Nepal and my Chateau in Heaven

I went in the spirit where Jesus was waiting for me in the same spot under a big tree.

I said, "Lord, I need You, I love You, I want more of You."

Jesus kissed my forehead and my palms and hugged me. He was wearing a crown of flowers and was laughing. He put a crown of flowers on my head also.

Jesus said, "Come, let's go. We have work to do."

We were then transported onto the streets somewhere in India. As we walked, there were people on each side of the road looking at us and smiling. We arrived at a hut where there was a man lying on the ground with dysentery. There were two healing angels assisting us. As we knelt down, I took my emerald green jar out and poured the healing oil over his head and body and then gave him some to drink that made him vomit. The man stood up and was healed completely. He came out rejoicing! Everyone was amazed praising God!

Jesus and I went further along to come upon a little girl that had only one leg. I asked Jesus, "What do you want me to do?"

He said, "Speak to the leg to grow out."

I went in the spirit to the body parts room of Heaven and saw a leg sitting on a shelf. I brought it back, spoke to the leg to grow out and it did in an instant! Wow! Powerful Almighty God!

She started walking and then running towards her mother in amazement. Her mom picked her daughter in her arms thanking Jesus.

Another time we went back to India where a group of hindus were going to stone ten Christians. The angels immediately surrounded them and their stones got suspended in the air and disappeared. When they saw the angels, they got scared and ran away. I took a yellowish liquid and poured it over the Christian's wounds and the wounds disappeared. One man in a wheelchair was healed. We took all the people to a safe place over the river.

Praise God for all miracles!

Healing in Nepal

Jesus and I went to Nepal. We walked on a mountain for a while then went inside a house where a widow was crying, saying her baby had died. We went to the other room where the baby was and Jesus told me to do CPR on the baby. I did five breaths and she started coughing, then crying. Her mother was shocked at this miracle, picked her up and shouted for joy. God is awesome and great!

Chapter 10

My Chateau in Heaven

Next, Jesus and I transported to Heaven. I asked Him to show me my chateau where I live. As I entered my chateau, inside was a huge waterfall that dropped into a pool. I saw many guardian angels surrounding us.

Jesus said, "Come upstairs."

There was a pink room and as I opened the door, I saw beautiful pink drapes surrounding the room. Wisdom lives here. This is so awesome!

I asked Jesus to take me to the Father's throne room. It was amazing scenery. The four faces of God (the Lion, Ox, Eagle and Man) were at each side of His throne.

I said, "Daddy, can I hug You please?"

He said, "Yes."

I sat on His lap where I got so filled with His presence, I didn't want to leave.

Then Father handed me a scroll. This is what was written on it," This is your destiny. I have great plans for you and Al. Get ready for a haul of blessings coming your way like a tidal wave. I AM. Soon you will move to your new house. Don't get distracted with this world. Healing is yours. Take it! Blessings are coming your way. Believe! Prophesy your future. Fast and pray as soon I am coming!"

Healing Aids and Cancer in Jerusalem

I continued my journey with Jesus in the spiritual realm. We walked through rivers passing over some stones and walked through a forest. We found a house on a top of a hill there was a mother with five kids living there. The kids were the following ages: five, six, seven, ten and twelve, all sick with aids and the mother had cancer.

Jesus gave me light, yellowish-green vials of liquid for the kids to drink. The vials were brought to us by healing angels that were made especially for them.

The first one, the five-year-old, was a girl; I gave her to drink, then the six-year-old, until all the kids drank. All of them got healed.

We gave two vials to the mother and she got healed from cancer. Praise God for these awesome miracles!

We went to the same square in Jerusalem we usually go to by a fountain. Jesus and I first saw a man walking with crutches. We approached him and asked what was wrong with his leg.

He said, "I broke my ankle." His leg was in a cast.

I asked him, "Would you like to have it healed?"

He said yes, "Go ahead."

I rebuked the pain in his ankle, I commanded the ligaments, bones, muscles and tendons to come into proper alignment with God's original design and be healed in Jesus' name.

I asked him, "How do you feel?"

He said, "It's amazing the pain in my ankle is completely gone."

I asked him to remove his cast and walk around. He did and walked back and forth with no pain whatsoever. He started to shout for joy.

Praise God!

The next person we encountered was a woman with her right arm in a cast. I asked her, "What happened to your arm?"

She said, "I broke it at work." She said it was painful.

I said, "Would you like to see this pain gone?"

"Yes, that would be great," she said.

I told her, "Jesus can heal any pain." Jesus was watching me as I commanded all the pain in the arm to leave, all the muscles, ligaments, tendons and bones to be healed in Jesus' name. After that I asked her, "Can you move your fingers, please?"

She started to move her fingers; then she took her cast off. I asked her to flex and extend her elbow. She did and she had great range of motion and no pain.

She said, "This is fantastic I have no more pain! Praise God!"

Journey with Jesus to the Himalayan Mountains

Jesus and I were walking at the bottom of the Himalayan Mountains. Many goats and sheep were roaming around. We came down a steep hill and to find a man dead on a rock. Jesus lifted His hand, spoke life into him and raised him from the dead.

We continued our journey to a house in the valley. There was a widow with five children. I saw a boy outside without a leg. I started to pray for the boy commanding the leg to grow. The metal leg disappeared and a new leg grew in its place. I saw a little girl without an eye. I put some drops from my green jar and an eyeball formed in the socket. We sat down at the table with the mother and she was astonished at these miracles. We gave her a Bible, told her about salvation and she received Jesus as her Savior.

When we finished, Jesus and I went to a ballroom in Heaven where there were many kings fellowshipping and dancing. I started dancing with Jesus. Al was present also. After a while, Father came and put medallions around our necks and took us to His throne room where He gave us a big key that we took, put inside a tall door that opened to show us our prayer mountain.

Diamonds for my Crown and a Ring

I went to the throne room and sat on the throne next to my Father. I was wearing my robe and crown.

Father and I began to dance until we formed a funnel and blended together; kings were also dancing and angels were playing instruments.

Jesus and I went to my garden where I opened a box that had two huge diamonds. Jesus took one of them and put it in my crown, the other one He smashed in small pieces and made a ring from them and put it on my finger.

Northwest Territories in Canada

Jesus and I traveled in the spirit to the Northwest Territories in Canada and met some indigenous people. Four men were chanting with incense, praying in their language and doing magic. They were doing this for a man that had a tumor inside of his chest. The warrior angel that was with us took a scepter in his hand and struck the ground making a loud noise, making all the occultic spirits to flee outside. The other angels took them in chains to prisons.

Jesus took the tumor out of the man like a surgery and sowed him back up. Everyone was shocked and amazed. I told them about salvation in Jesus and that He died on the cross for them and that He is the only true God. The man that got healed got up and sat in a chair fellowshipping with us.

Praise God for another healing miracle.

Walking in the Garden of Eden

Father, Jesus and I went to the Garden of Eden. Elephants and other animals were walking around. I saw angels with white robes coming towards us. One of them gave me a bow and arrows and I practiced shooting arrows on a target. We went further to a camp where lots of warrior angels were practicing with their weapons.I was wearing full armor and I had shield. My warrior angels were wearing shoulder pads and full armor.

We all mounted our horses and went to battle a beast with multiple heads. This beast was above a village tormenting people. I cut off one of the heads with my fiery sword. I held my shield up as one of them threw fire at me. There were many angels battling this beast.

One of the angels threw what looked like a rocket and the entire body of the beast exploded. The body fell to the ground making a loud noise. Lots of angels with swords were fighting many other small dragons on the ground. I went down with my horse Isaiah and cut into the middle of its belly. Hundreds of small diamonds that fell out of the beast I exchanged for a golden scroll at the sea of glass.

Healing in Africa - June 2, 2013

I traveled in the spirit with Al to a platform in Africa where we were having a conference. Al was speaking to the crowd where miracles, signs and wonders were taking place among the people. One woman came on the stage without a leg. Al and I prayed for her and the leg grew out instantly. Praise God! He can do this with faith! Then another woman came out on the stage without an arm and her arm grew out. Praise God what a miracle!

Lepers healed

I was with Jesus sitting by a fire. He was poking a stick into the flames. I asked Him if we could go heal someone.

A chariot of angles came, picked us up and we traveled to a village. A man came towards us who was possessed by many demons. Jesus cast

them all out and angels took them away in chains to a spiritual prison.

We walked into a village to see an elderly lady without a leg from the knee down.

I said, "Lord, she needs a leg."

Jesus said, "Go and heal her."

An angel took me to the body parts room in Heaven to look for a leg for this woman. There were so many shelves with body parts everywhere. I found a suitable leg and brought it back to this woman, and put it on her. Her Heavenly leg formed onto her. She instantly noticed what happened and started jumping up-and-down for joy, praising the Lord!

Jesus said, "Let's go further, we've got work to do."

We arrived at a leper colony, where there was a hut full of people. The stench was so bad, that angels came to disperse the smell for me. Jesus poured a liquid over my head and body to keep me protected from this disease. There were a total of twenty lepers in the hut. As Jesus and I entered the hut, He took a beautiful emerald vial and poured its contents over some of the lepers. The Lord then gave me the vial to pour it over the rest of them. All of them got instantly healed! They all came out of the hut shouting and praising God for this miracle!

The Golden Scroll

I went with my sweetheart Jesus into my heart garden by our usual tree. I went around the tree and as I circled the tree it grew taller and higher than a sequoia tree.

Jesus said to me, "Look inside the branches what do you see?"

"I see a fruit that looks like a papaya," I said.

I gave one to Jesus, Who cut it in half taking out a diamond the size of a walnut.

He took another fruit and took out a ruby, then another one that was an emerald, then a topaz, a blue diamond, jasper and zirconium. He put all of them in a basket and said let's go. We were transported to a waterfall with high cliffs. We went down some rocks all the way down to the waterfall, crossed over and started to climb up the other side of the cliff until we reached a very steep gap.

I said, "Lord, how are we going to cross there is no bridge."

Jesus took all the precious stones, threw them and they became a multicolored bridge. We crossed over, reaching a cave. There was a black snake inside which I killed with my sword. When we arrived in front of a big wall, one angel struck it and a wave of diamonds, rubies and emeralds dropped out. The angels took all of the diamonds and stored them in a sack.

Jesus stretched out His hand and took out a box; opened it and took out a small golden key. The key was very shiny and bright.

He said, "Take this key and open this door." He pointed to the door next to us.

I opened the door that had many shelves and on each shelf were scrolls. We took all the scrolls to the Court of Scribes to be recorded.

I said, "Lord what are all these scrolls?"

He said, "They represent seasons in your life."

"Can I read one?"

He took one of the golden scrolls, opened it, which was like a movie showing Al at a lake where a huge crowd followed him. Al was teaching the crowd.

I said, "Is this what I think it is Lord."

He said, "Yes. It's the prayer mountain."

I said, "Awesome Lord."

He then rolled the scroll back up and said, "Eat the scroll," which I did making my entire body become like gold dust.

Praise God for the miracles and all He has in store for us and may His destiny for us be fulfilled in Jesus name. Amen!

Traveling to Namibia

Jesus and I traveled to Namibia to a house where a blind woman lived. She had fallen on the floor and hit her head. Jesus and I were standing in front of her. I was holding a bandage to her head. Jesus told me to look at her eyes and He said, "Call that which is not there."

I commanded the eyes to form in her sockets and two brown eyes formed. The woman screamed and shouted for joy. The first person she would see in her life was Jesus Yeshua Hamashiach!

Praise God for this miracle.

Raising the Dead in Rwanda and Healing in Norway

I was walking behind Jesus, following in His footsteps. We climbed up a rock on the beach and gazed out at the sea.

I said, "Lord, I want more of You. I want to go other countries and do healings and raise the dead."

We traveled in the spirit to a village hut in Murindi, Rwanda, Africa. I saw a woman lying on the floor dead.

Jesus said, "Lay hands on her."

As I did that I said, "Get up in Jesus name!" The woman got up and was astonished at this miracle. She walked out of the hut and was dancing and praising the Lord.

Jesus and I entered a building where there was a group of people concerned for this woman who was lying on a mat. Jesus told me to blow life into her, I did and she rose from the dead.

After that we went a long distance through woods to a house where smoke was coming out of the chimney. We were in Norway.

Jesus and I entered to see three people surrounding the bed where a woman in a long white garment was lying down on a bed. She had a terrible fever. Jesus approached her and told me to take this oil and massage her hands arms and face. After a while the fever left completely and she stood up and walked around.

Healing in Jerusalem Again

Jesus and I were transported to Jerusalem. We walked through a field past some sheep. Ahead of us was a dead man. I knew he had been dead for five days.As we knelt down next to him, Jesus touched his forehead as I poured some oil over his head. Then he suddenly stood up and walked away praising God for this miracle.

Next, we went to a market with many people. We approached a woman who had her arm in a cast with a sling. We asked her what happened to her arm. She said she broke it. Jesus spoke these words, "Be healed." The cast just fell off. Jesus asked her to move and flex her arm. It was completely healed. She was shouting praises to God. After that, we saw a little girl limping on her left leg.

Jesus said to me, "This is your gig now, she has a sprain."

I approached the girl and I asked her if she would let me pray for her. She nodded yes. I rebuked the strained ligaments and joints and commanded the foot to straighten out. It did, and she started to walk with no pain. She was so amazed she ran over to her mother rejoicing.

Jesus heals my Mother's Leg

I went to the courts of Heaven and pled the case for my mother leg.

I said, "Lord, my mom's been in bondage with lots of illness for many years. I want her to be healed." I saw my mom in a corner shivering. Satan was accusing her that she hangs on to her fear.

Jesus told the accuser to go as she is my child.

Satan said he had a right to her because she's fearful.

I saw a long chain tied to her leg.

I said to the devil, "Let her go." I almost struck him with my sword but Jesus stopped me.

Jesus turned to my mom and asked her, "Do you believe that I am with you always? You don't need to be afraid. Do you believe that I am your healer?"

My mom said, "Lord, I believe."

Then Jesus commanded the angels to break the chains and they cut them with their swords. My mom was free.

As she sat down, Jesus poured oil over her leg saying, "Come to Me every day and drink from Me. I paid the price for you on the cross to be set free. Believe, don't doubt, I am with you."

Several days later my mom told me that her leg was healed. She wasn't aware that I had gone in the spirit with Jesus to do this miracle.

Praise God to Him be the glory!

Jesus and I Journey to Thailand

We walked on a busy street with lots of people around to a small house behind a building. There was a man sick with tuberculosis lying on the floor. He was spitting up blood. Jesus told me to cast out the demon and when I started, the demon said that it had a right to stay.

I asked the man, "Do you know Jesus."

He said, "No who's He?"

I said, "He is the one who died for your sins on the cross, repent and receive Him as your Savior. Do you want to receive Him as your Savior?"

He said, "Yes."

So, I led him in prayer of repentance and salvation and after that I cast out the demon. My warrior angel took it to a spiritual prison. The man coughed several times and was fully restored and free. He got up, sat at the table and ate.

DNA

I went with Jesus and Father by a beautiful waterfall where doves were flying around. Jesus and I became white eagles; flew above the waterfall; landed on a tree branch; went behind the waterfall into a cave to a wall where Jesus scraped off some gold and put it in sacks. Angels took the sacks to my finance mountain.

I went to the bridal chamber where angels poured water over me purifying me, and then He clothed me in a new golden robe and a new crown. I sat on a table and Father did a bone marrow transplant to change my DNA.

I was taken to the library of Heaven and shown a big scroll about what Al and I will do in the future for the Kingdom of God; places where we'd travel and reach many people doing deliverance, healings, etc.

Jesus and I went to Jerusalem, walking on a narrow street and entered a building. Upstairs was a boy with aids. When Jesus did a transfusion of his blood and DNA he was healed completely.

Sitting on Daddy's lap - August, 30 2017

I went in the spirit to Father's Chambers and fell down at His feet.

I said "Father, Daddy I would like to see Your face."

Father asked me to come and sit on His lap. I hesitated, but Jesus was there also, so He encouraged me to go forward. I sat on Father's lap. It was an amazing feeling, sitting in His presence.

Next I went to a waterfall. As I was swimming, I put my hand under the waterfall and there were diamonds, white sparkling diamonds, in my hand.

I went up onto the beach where Jesus was looking at a map.

He said, "We are going to Israel today."

We went inside of a building in Jerusalem where there was a woman lying in a bed with sores. I poured a liquid on her that I had and watched as her sores disappeared. She was so amazed at this miracle she got up dancing and rejoicing.

Then Jesus and I went to another place through some gates where there was a woman who was dead in her bed surrounded by multitudes of people. As Jesus spoke life into her, she got up and rose from the dead.

Praise the Lord!

Adventures with my King in Capernaum and Jericho

Jesus and I went boat fishing. We threw a net in the water and caught lots of fish.We took the fish up on the beach, cut them and put them in buckets.

When we got back on the boat, Jesus said, "We are going now to northern Israel."

We sailed across to the other side of the Sea of Galilee to land in Capernaum. We walked to an area that had streets of cobblestone. Jesus told me to start preaching the gospel.

I stood on a stool and started to preach, "On these very streets walked a King whom you have rejected and crucified, the King, Jesus Christ the Son of God. Come to Him now and repent and have your sins washed away, and be purified. He is coming back again. Don't let God find you without repentance. He can heal any sickness and disease in your body."

A man in the crowd was laughing, saying, "If He is the Son of God and He is the One you say He is; how can my brother still be sick from cancer. He has been suffering for a long time?"

I said, "Jesus can heal him right now. Bring him here." Then I said, "No, in fact I am going to go to him now in the spirit."

I traveled in the spirit and I saw a man lying on his bed dressed with dark clothes. I commanded every cell in his body to be regenerated new and the cancer ones to die. A fire sparked burning his body until all the cancer cells disappeared. He was completely cured. I said to the man, "Jesus has healed you."

I went back in the spirit to the crowd and said, "Your brother is healed."

The man still didn't believe until he received a phone call. "What?" he said.His brother said to him, "I am healed. I have no more cancer."

The man was astonished and said: "Really? I don't believe you. I am going to take you to the doctor right now and do tests."

"O you of little faith why did you doubt?" Jesus said in Matthew 14:31.

As the man left, another man without a leg came close to us. I commanded the leg to grow and it did. Then two men in wheelchairs got up and were healed also. I looked at the crowd and said, "Now, who wants to receive Jesus as their Savior?"

All of them put their hands up and received Jesus as their Savior!

Jesus said, "We need to cross over to where the Palestinians are."

I said, "Lord is it safe?"

He replied, "You are always safe with Me." Jesus said, "There is a man here who is confused about his faith. I appeared to him in his dreams many times, but he still hasn't decided to follow Me. I want you to tell him about Me."

So, we went to this man's house. As he opened the door I said, "I know about your dreams regarding Jesus. He is real don't doubt in your heart." I gave him a Bible. "Everything you need to know about Yeshua is here in this Book." The man hesitated. I told him that Jesus is here with me.

When I said that, Jesus appeared to him and said, "I am the Way, The Truth and The Life, anyone who comes to Me shall not perish but have eternal life, believe in Me, follow Me."

The man fell down at His feet. Jesus said, "Repent now and receive Me as your Lord and Savior."

The man repented and he was baptized in the Dead Sea. I also laid my hands on him and he received the baptism of the Holy Spirit.

These were my adventures with Father and Jesus on this day! Praise the Lord Jesus Yeshua Hamashiach!

Healing people of Malaria in Africa

I went to the Bridal Chambers where angels were fitting my bride dress that was white with a golden robe and crown. I sat in my governmental seat of authority on the right hand of my Father. What an honor to sit next to Him, also next to my King of kings and Lord of lords.

Jesus and I went to Africa. I was pumping water out of a well to a lot of kids that were lined up. One of them had a pain in his left leg. I approached him, rebuked the pain and he started to walk normally. He was jumping up and down with joy.

Jesus and I approached a boy lying dead. I looked at Jesus and He said, "You know what to do."

I rebuked the spirit of death and commanded the life of Christ to come into this body. The boy coughed and he rose from the dead. Praise God for this resurrection! After that Jesus said, "Follow me."

We went inside a hut and there were five people lying on mats sick with malaria. I give them some white pills. Jesus also asked me to give them to drink from green vials. When I did, they all coughed and were healed completely. Praise God!

Jesus and I continued our journey to a beach by a river. We encamped there and ate fish. It was so good to fellowship with the Lord.

He said, "Stay away from distractions, seek Me first and fast."

"Ok Lord," I said.

Adventures in Zambia

Next day we crossed a bridge by a waterfall. Jesus told me that we were in Zambia. There are two tribes here that are at war. We sent warrior angels to the camp were the tribes were. Jesus said we can go now to meet them. One of the leaders of the tribe had a spear in his hand and wanted to kill the other leader in the tribe but he stopped and said, "There is something in the atmosphere."

Jesus and I approached them. I said, "We came in peace." I asked him, "Have you ever heard of Jesus."

He said, "No, who's he?" "He is the King of kings and Lord of Lords."

He pointed the spear towards us. I said, "Your daughter is sick, isn't she?"

He said, "How did you know that?"

I said, "I saw a vision about your daughter lying down sick. If you let me pray for her, I can guarantee that Jesus will heal her." The leader hesitated. I said, "Ok let's make a deal, if your daughter gets healed, you and your men will receive Jesus as their Lord and Savior, if not, you can kill us." He agreed.

We went to a hut where a girl was sick with malaria and pneumonia. Jesus gave me a small box that had shimmery dust in it. He said, "Spread this all over her body." I did that and also took my emerald green jar and poured oil over her body massaging her. After a while the girl opened her eyes, got up and started to walk.

She looked at her father and said, "I'm hungry." She was given food to eat. All of the people marveled at this miracle.

The leader fell down and worshipped Jesus. Jesus touched his head and prayed for him. They all received Jesus as their Savior, received Bibles and were baptized in the river. Praise God!

Court of Galactic Counsel of Seventy

Al and I went to the Court of Galactic Counsel of Seventy. Here there are records regarding nations. We were sitting in the audience. They summoned us by name and gave us a scroll to take to the Court of Chancellors who stamped it. On a table there was a sack full of gold coins. I asked Jesus how do we take these to the physical realm.

He said, "It will be put into our account. You will go to the nations."

Cleaning Gateways

I went into my garden where Jesus was waiting for me by the river lying on a white sheet. We had a picnic and ate fish, bread and had wine.

He said to me, "Soak into my presence, I AM, this world does not offer you what I give you."

While we fellowshipped and ate, I went to my gateways to clean them up. I engaged the love gate first where a bright light soaked my entire body in the light and presence of the Lord until every fibre of my being started to vibrate. In my subconscious gate there were spider webs that Jesus removed. My warrior angels removed two familiar spirits and took them out of the gate. I pled the blood and covered the entire gateway with the blood of Jesus and closed and sealed the door tight.

I went to my conscious and emotion gateways and did the same thing cleaning out and applying the blood of Jesus.

At my body gateway I took my sword and cut out a familiar spirit who had a chain hooked into the gateway and my warrior angels took out some snakes. I took a brush and painted my entire gateway with the blood of Jesus and closed tight the door. I asked for a warrior angel with a fiery sword to guard this gateway.

I went back to the garden where Father joined us at a table to fellowship with us. I was in three places at the same time: soaking in the light, cleaning the gateways and having a picnic with Father and Jesus.

After the picnic Jesus and I crossed a river. He took a rock with unusual light-blue edges, broke it and shaped it until a beautiful translucent gem stone diamond with many facets formed.

Chapter 10

He took the diamond and put it into my crown.

Healing in Jordan

I went traveling in the spirit with Jesus where this time we crossed over to Jordan.We went inside a house where a woman was physically abused by her husband. She had a big wound on her right arm and a black eye. Jesus touched her arm as I poured oil over it and the wound instantly disappeared. The woman was scared and backed into the corner of the room.

I calmed her down and told her that this is the King of kings and Lord of lords Who died on the cross for her sins so that she will be forgiven and set free.

Jesus said, "Don't be afraid my daughter for I came to rescue you and heal you. Follow me and you shall have eternal life."

I also gave her a Bible. She then hugged Jesus and received Him in her life. Angels took her to a rescue house for women.

Jesus and I crossed back to Israel to Nazareth and went inside a hospital. An orthodox Jew was there with a leg injury. A car hit him on the road and left him with a bad wound. His leg was in a cast up to his hip. He was in a lot of pain. I saw an angel cutting the cast open and then Jesus poured liquid and oil over the wound. The man was sleeping while he did this.

Then the Lord spoke to his conscience. He said, "Isaac, I AM the beginning and the end. You searched all of your life for answers but you could not find them. I died on the cross for you. Believe in Me, follow Me."

The man woke up to see Jesus and was so shocked he couldn't say anything. He stood up, not realizing his leg was totally healed. He walked around the room afraid of what his family were going to do to him if he follows Jesus.

The Lord said, "Don't be afraid."

Then it hit him. He looked at his leg and marveled at this miracle healing.

He fell at Jesus' feet saying, "Adonai! You are indeed the Son of God."

After a while this man's family walked in and they were shocked to see he was absolutely healed. He started telling them what happened and how Jesus healed him.

Praise God for victory in Jesus.

Another Journey to India to Raise the Dead

Jesus and I traveled in India to do miracles. We walked for a while on a road until we arrived at a village. There were many people dying from diseases. I suspected that we would be raising people from the dead. Warrior angels accompanied us. We asked the people around us to take ten bodies and lay them next to each other on the ground.

Jesus told me to put my hand on each of them and say, "Get up in the name of Jesus."

When I did as I was instructed all of them rose one by one into a line. Jesus walked by each of them and gave them their scrolls of destiny.

I preached the gospel to them saying, "This is Jesus the Son of God who died for your sins on the cross. Follow Him."

Meeting Moses and David

I went to Heaven and met Moses who gave me a scroll.

He said, "With faith you can move mountains."

David gave me a dagger that I put on my side.

Four Doors - May 9, 2019

I went to a waterfall with four streams of water that covered four doors behind them.

I entered the first door walking with Jesus through a corridor to a chair where I sat. Angels brought me gifts. An angel brought frankincense and prompted me to follow him to the soaking room to be soaked in it.

I went through the second door to see a crown ornate with large jewels, red, purple, topaz, jasper and onyx. Then I went to the Father's throne room where we walked from there to the Garden of Eden that had many animals, oceans, mountains and waterfalls.

The third door had men in white linen: Jeremiah, Isaiah, David and Solomon. They each gave me a scroll. I went to the library of Heaven and opened the scroll that Jeremiah gave me where it was written, "Fire like comes out of your mouth to burn people like wood."

"Because you [the people] have spoken this word, behold, I will make My words fire in your mouth [Jeremiah] and this people wood, and it will devour them." Jeremiah 5:14

On Isaiah's scroll was written, "Faithfulness and Steadfastness."

Solomon's said, "Take this to the record room." The scroll was white with a red ribbon.I opened the scroll and it was written, "Wisdom beyond your imagination; wisdom like Solomon." I took the scroll to the record room and angels recorded it. The angels told me to take it to the Court of Chancellors where authorizations of mandates, laws and legislations are made. Scrolls brought here must be sealed by a chancellor. Many times, papers that are received in the mobile court also need to be sealed by a chancellor. A cloud of witnesses was present here.

David also gave me an unusual looking scroll made of leather that was grayish and brown. It was a battle scroll. When I opened the scroll, I saw a black horse. I was on my black horse Jordan followed by an army of angels battling snakes, dragons and hydras. After we killed them all with our swords, warrior angels gathered them up and threw them into another dimension. The ground where the battle took place sprung up with diamonds, emeralds and jasper.

I entered through the fourth door where Jesus gave me a scroll. This scroll unrolled into multi-cascades of waterfalls that were connected by several bridges. The scenery was indescribable. I was surrounded by these magnificent waterfalls that dropped over five miles below where Jesus and I were standing on a bridge.

I asked Him about the scroll and He said, "This scroll is frequency, vibration and the sound of Heaven. This is what connects you all the time. Remain in this."

The Red Robe and The Red Crown

I went into Heaven to my favorite place, the big waterfall, where Jesus and I were swimming in the water, splashing and having fun. After that I went to the bridal chambers and received a red robe, red crown and a red scroll.

Jesus told me to take the scroll to the Court of Kings to have it recorded.

Nepal

Jesus and I traveled to Nepal. We walked many streets and went over many hills. We entered a house where a warlock lived who was sick. Jesus told me to give him to drink from a red vial. After he drank from it a snake came out of him. Angels put it into a sack. When I gave him to drink from a purple vial, frogs came out of him. The last one he drank was from a yellow vial and locusts came out of him. He got delivered completely with manifestation of screaming.

I asked him, "Do you renounce and give up witchcraft?"

He said, "Yes."

"Do you accept Jesus as your Lord and Savior?"

He said, "Yes."

Jesus blessed him while an angel poured oil over him. We also baptized him in a river. He took all his books and witchcraft objects and burned them.

Praise God for freedom!

The Garden of Eden

I went to my heart garden where Jesus was waiting for me. We walked through the river and picked up a bright multicolored gem that was light pink, blue and red. We went to the sea of glass and exchanged it for a fiery scroll. I took the scroll to the Court of Kings.On this scroll was written names of nations: Nigeria, Philippines, Thailand, India and Australia.

I went to the Garden of Eden and met the Father where we walked around. A lion approached us. I caressed the lion. The lion and I played in a field. One of the four faces of God is the Lion and symbolizes strength, stamina, power and domination. Father told me that this lion will be with me at all times. The Lord told me to eat the fiery scroll which I did.

Jesus and I traveled to Thailand. The lion was with us. We approached a house where a woman was persecuted for her faith by her husband. Her husband had a weapon in his hand. When the lion roared the weapon fell out of his hand. My warrior angels restrained the man and we took the woman out of the house to a safe location. I gave her water to drink.

Another Journey to Nepal

Jesus and I approached a house that had lots of goats in front of it. We went inside where a woman was kneeling at a bed where another woman was sick with a blood disease. Jesus called in angels to bring an IV and He put the IV in her arm, to purify her blood. I took my emerald green jar and massaged her forearms while Jesus gave her some pills. I could see the liquid, from my emerald jar, produced electric currents that was cleaning her blood. She was healed completely. She got up and hugged Jesus. We gave her a Bible before we left.

Journeys in the spirit are awesome because among other reasons, I lay hands on the sick in the spirit and they recover quickly. The methods that Jesus shows me are fantastic. When they live in another country, I go in the spirit and raise the dead and heal the sick. All things are possible by faith being translated by faith in the spiritual realm. In the spirit, doubt and unbelief does not exist like in the natural realm.In the spiritual realm you are aware of your authority, so I really don't have time to think about doubt. It all happens fast. Jesus and I are doing miracles fast.

Jesus and I Journey to China

Jesus and I traveled to China walking by a forest on a street where some soldiers were getting ready to stone and kill five Christians. When they threw the stones at them, the stones became sand and fell to the ground. Angels surrounded the soldiers and made themselves visible to them. The soldiers got scared and ran away into the forest. Jesus threw an invisible blanket over the Christians and translated them to a safe house.

Jesus and I went to another place in China where ten Christians were about to get shot. We were surrounded by six mighty angels. When the soldiers fired, the bullets ricocheted around. Some of the bullets became dust. The soldiers were shocked and didn't know what was happening.

All of us got translated to a safe house by a river in mountains, specifically Yarlung Zangbo River by Mount Kailash in Tibet, where Jesus gave them a road map to continue their journey to safety.

Another time we found a group of Christians that had been persecuted and tortured for their faith, locked up in a short, wooden box with wooden bars, laying on the floor bleeding. I took my emerald green jar and poured liquid over a woman's wounds, massaging her arms and legs. Her wounds disappeared. I did the same for the rest of the people. I told them that Jesus is Yeshua HaMashiach and they all started worshiping the Lord. We broke them out and went to a forest and then to a field with flowers where they hid at a safe house.

Healing in Florida

I went in the spirit with Jesus to Carol's house. She was in her living room sitting on the couch with one leg up on another chair. (She had a torn meniscus and pain in her knee from a fall). As I poured liquid from my emerald green jar over her knee, I saw an angel with a tray approach us. He came close to Carol and pulled six big nails out of her knee. He put the nails on the tray and left. Another angel came to bandage her leg. I released the light of Christ into her knees and poured oil over her head. I asked her to walk around to activate her faith. She got up slowly at first, as she used a walker, but then she pushed it away.

After that Jesus touched her head and said, "Blessed are you my daughter among women, you've been faithful. Continue in faith my daughter. A new season of blessings are coming to you. Faith will sustain you. I AM. Come to me daily; spend time with Me in the spirit."

Then He turned to John her husband and said, "Blessed are you John a warrior for Christ. Your heart pleases Me. Stay on the narrow path. I AM. Don't be discouraged. I will take you to where you need to be. I am holding your hand steadily on this path."

Testimony from Carol came later: She was completely healed. Praise God!

Journey to Turkey

I went to my garden where Jesus, wearing a white robe, was waiting for me under a tree. He put a crown of flowers on my head; gave me a key and a dagger; put a veil over my head and asked me to drink a bowl of liquid that an angel brought.

We then took a journey to Turkey to a house where a woman was beaten by her husband. Immediately the warrior angels surrounded the woman to protect her.Her husband saw the angels and fainted. Jesus and I took the woman and laid her on the bed. I took a white bottle out from a pouch that I was wearing on my side and poured it over her wounds. The wounds closed immediately and she was healed. I also did deliverance on her and she got set free. We translocated her to a safe-house in another city where she received help by other Christian women.

Jesus, Father and I went to a beach to skip stones on the water. Al joined us and all of us had a picnic on the beach. Father gave Al a scroll that he put in his mantle. Jesus opened a blue box that had a blue diamond on a silver chain that He put around my neck.

I went to the dance floor dancing with Jesus, Father and Holy Spirit. We all became intertwined like a small funnel. Dancing with Jesus and the Father is the place of intimacy and is also when we begin to take the image of sonship by engaging the character and the nature of God.

Joshua came to give me a scroll which was written: "Nigeria."

At the Father's chambers, Al's five ancient ones (angels) together with my other three angels walked in. Al received three scrolls: a red, blue and a green one. I received three scrolls also: orange, yellow and a pink one.

On the pink scroll it said: "Precious daughter you have a special gift to reach out to hurting woman. This scroll is anointed for love, mercy and wisdom."

On the orange scroll was written: "Spirit of Wisdom. More wisdom will be given to you. I saw Wisdom given me to drink something like honey.

Raising the dead in Switzerland

After that we went to the Father's chambers and sat by the fireplace. Angels brought lemon cookies and tea. Al was there also talking about a scroll with Father. The door opened and warrior angels wearing multicolored robes came in with special elite angels. Al received a new dagger. An angel gave me a new golden bright sword. Al received a red robe and a new red scroll from Father. Al got on a black horse and left for a battle on the top of a mountain.

I went traveling with Jesus to Switzerland to the Alps and on the top of one mountain was a frozen man. We dug him up, Jesus laid hands on him and the man defrosted immediately and was raised from the dead.

Journey to Gaza

I went to the bridal chambers where Jesus was dressing me with green garments and I was wearing a crown with shiny, sparkling, green stones. I danced with Jesus and Father on the dance floor.

I went to the Father's throne room and cast my crown before Him. He put it back on my head and I sat next to Him on my throne. The four faces of God were there and I looked at the eagle face. The eagle came close and danced around me.

Then Father became a big, majestic eagle and I became a white eagle and we flew around doing accolades in the air, diving next to a waterfall. I went swimming with Jesus in the waterfall. Everything was serene bright shining light.

Jesus and I went walking on a pathway. He said, "Today we are going to Gaza to minister to some people."

We went through an arched entrance into a house, where a muslim man was bowing down to the floor reciting endless prayers. His wife was sick with cancer and she was dying. We moved closer to where the woman was laying. The man looked at Jesus and was shocked because my Lord was in a different form, full of bright light.

Jesus asked him, "Do you believe I can heal your wife?"

The man said, "Who are you?"

Jesus replied, "I am the Way. The Truth and The life, Follow Me."

The man said, "Help my wife please. I believe."

Jesus then touched the woman and she was immediately restored to health. Jesus instructed both to eat bread and drink. They both did and the woman got up from bed amazed at her miracle.

Praise God for her healing!

We gave them a Bible. Jesus said to the man, "Go preach the gospel to many."

The man took the Bible and went to preach the gospel in his village.

Healing a man on a Beach

I was in the spirit and went under my tree in the garden where Jesus was waiting for me. Jesus and I had fellowship for a while and after that He said, "Come, let's take a stroll."

So, we walked through the trees and jumped into a river and floated until we arrived at a waterfall.

I said, "Wait a minute. This is the waterfall that we swim at all the time. Wow! This is in my garden Lord?" Jesus smiled and nodded.

We swam for a while playing in the water. We dove under the water and swam for a while until we got to a beach. We saw a man breathing very hard.

I asked, "Lord, how are we going to heal him." I looked inside of his heart to see a blockage. Jesus removed the blockage and he was healed.

After that Jesus and I went to my house in Hawaii (spiritual). We sat on the deck admiring the ocean.

I said, "This is mine Lord?"

He said, "Yes." Jesus then said, "If you think this is beautiful, wait until I show you this." So, we went to a similar place where there were mountains that were green and made of diamonds that was alive with a beach next to it where Father joined us.

A group of warrior angels came and gave me a scroll. There were special elite angels with unusual armour on; shoulder pads all leather and, multicolored robes. I looked at Jesus thinking, "Battle?"

He nodded.

Then, out in the ocean I saw a twister coming up from the bottom of the ocean into the sky. The angels and I were on our horses surrounding this twister when a head came out. I struck it with my sword and cut if off. The angels attacked it with bow and arrows. The battle was intense. Fire from Heaven came down and destroyed it. Its remains were taken into a different dimension.

I was summoned to go to the Court of Angels, where all of us received medallions.

When I was in Hawaii, Jesus and I visited some native Hawaiians. There was a house where people were concerned about a relative dying inside the house. Jesus and I passed by them. They didn't see us. There was a huge man sitting on the bed who I knew had congestive heart failure. I saw a cobra coming out of him. Warrior angels were also in the room. When I cut its head off more snakes came out. Angels put them into a bag and took them away. We did warfare until all the snakes were taken out.

The man asked Jesus, "Who are you?"

I said, "This is Jesus Who died on the cross for you to wash away your sins."

Jesus showed him a vision when He was on the cross and how His blood paid for his sins.

I said, "Would you like to receive Him as your Savior?"

He said, "Yes I will." We gave Him a Bible. He repented. We took him to a pond and he was baptized.

Praise God for all the Glory and Victory!

Communion with Father on the Beach

I went to a beautiful beach in Heaven with Jesus where He threw balls of light at me. Angels came with Moses, Enoch and Bob Jones. He gave me a scroll and I ate it. Enoch gave me a book: wisdom and knowledge and a key to unlock mysteries.
Father and Al came and we all had communion on the beach.

Three Scrolls - September 17, 2019

Al and I went to a beach to walk with Father, Jesus, angels and our ancient ones where we received three scrolls.

One was golden, another one silver and the last one was platinum.

The first scroll had the title "destiny", the second one said "assignment" and third one said "declaration."

Al and I then went to the throne room and received golden mantles.

Clothed with the Spirit of Wisdom

I went to the bridal chambers where Jesus was purifying me with water.

He said, "Today you will be clothed with orange, the Spirit of Wisdom."

He gave me orange garments and we went to dance on the dance floor. I went to the throne room and bowed down before my Father and cast my crown. The four faces of God came close and we danced. I did a twirl with the eagle. I put my forehead against the ox and the lion was roaring, I hugged him and we started to walk in the garden. I went to the Father's chambers by the fireplace. Al was there also. I saw Isaiah and the men in white linen, who gave Al a book.

It was written, "You shall be great among people. You are sealed with the blood of Jesus. Mountains shall be moved. The way is paved. Walk in it. Doors are opening."

Then I saw Al's mother Lynn. We all had a great time fellowshipping. Angels brought us lemon cookies. I saw Bob Jones laying hands on Al and blessing him.

Making Crowns with Jesus for Saints

I went to the river in my garden where Jesus and I were both swimming. The light of the Father came upon us and it was very bright. Jesus took out a rock from the water that had rubies around it. He chopped all the dark parts out and put all the rubies in a basket to go to my finance mountain. The diamond-cutter angel took the rubies and made them into facet-shaped rubies, filling out twenty baskets of rubies.

The angels took the baskets to a white table and we made crowns for saints.

Jesus put red rubies in the crowns and trimmed them with gold and silver. Some crowns were decorated with emeralds. After that we went to the governmental seat where I sat next to Father and Jesus. What an honor to serve the Kings of kings and Lord of lords. As we sat in our seat of authority, we distributed crowns to the saints as they were standing in a queue. We also gave them a scepter and scrolls of destiny.

We took this group of saints to Eden where we took the Lord's communion. It was a party in Heaven!

Five scrolls

I went to my heart garden where Jesus took me to a big, black tree. He said this has to be uprooted. I saw angels pushing the tree down, with the roots showing and the angels lifted it out and threw it away.

Jesus brought five fire scrolls to burn all the seeds in the ground around this tree. Those seeds were: fear, disappointment, anxiety and deception.

Journey to Hong Kong

I went into my heart garden where Jesus and I planted flowers. Jesus planted a big white diamond in the ground that grew into a tree that was full of diamonds. When I spoke, multicolored flowers of yellow, purple lavender and jasmine sprouted up. I went on the dance floor where Jesus put an emerald in my crown and all my garments became green. The Spirit of Counsel was all over me.

Jesus and I went to a beach and we found four people dead.

The first one rose when Jesus said, "Arise" in Hebrew.

The second one I poured from my emerald green jar in his mouth and he rose from dead.

215

The third one and the fourth one I said," Get up in Jesus name," and they did. Jesus gave each of them a scroll.

We went back in time to Hong Kong inside a house where a mother of five kids was sick in bed dying. Jesus took some tools from His bag and operated on her. After He finished the woman was completely healed. All the kids were happy and surrounded her.

Dancing with Father and Jesus again

I went to the dance floor where I was wearing my priestly robes that had silver with gold trim. Jesus was so royal, crowned with a beautiful golden crown decorated with red, blue and purple jewels. I was dancing with the Father also.

I went into my garden and I followed Jesus to a river bank where there was a stone rock that was silvery and black. We passed through a river on the other side, walked over some hills to arrive in a valley. I saw in the distance a group of people with dark skin waiting for us to come and minister to them. When we arrived, Jesus gave them Bibles.

I asked the Lord, "Who are these people Lord?"

Jesus said, "They are hungry for Me, I shall heal their hearts."

I saw an angel throwing what looked like plastic wrap over them as a protection against the virus.

Jesus gave them to drink from fluorescent vials and they all got healed.

Traveling to see a Government Official in China

Jesus and I continued our journey on a road to a fancy house in China. The house belonged to a rich person from the government of China.

Jesus said to me, "My children have been persecuted way too long here in this land."

We went inside this house where a government leader was looking over a map with other men. They were looking at South East China at a camp where many Christians were being held captive. They could not see us and I could understand what they were saying.

The leader said, "We must kill fifty Christians."

Jesus took a drop of oil from His pouch and put it on this man's head. The man looked back at the map and said that they are not going to kill them.

Another man asked him, "What do you mean we are not going to kill them?"

He replied, "Not at the moment."

After that we were at a prison camp in South East China by the South China Sea. We were accompanied by five big angels. The angels opened the doors and went behind the guards opening the doors to the fifty Christians. All of them came out and followed us as we took them across the border to Vietnam and then into Cambodia. We gave them sacks of food and they went on their way. Praise God!

I went to the Father's chambers by the fireplace. Angels were giving us cookies and tea as Father gave Al and I each a scroll. A thirty-foot warrior angel came in and took Al with him to a battle. The warrior angel was like a giant gladiator with a breast-plate, huge sword and roman sandals. At the battle, a huge python was slithering around and around, taunting them. The angel took the beast in his arms and stretched it out. Al took his sword and cut its head off.

Praise God for all the victory.

Three Hundred Glasses of Diamonds

I went under a tree in my garden where Jesus was waiting for me. He was wearing a white-linen robe with a bright, white hood. We hugged for a long time with my head against His chest, feeling at peace in Him. After a while we walked through the river collecting beautiful white diamonds

into many sacks. Angels put them on a chariot and brought them to my finance mountain. Jesus asked the angels to make liquid out of the diamonds and pour them in glasses that looked like champagne glasses.

Jesus said, "Drink it all. This will protect you from the virus."

Al joined me and we both drank all three-hundred glasses with this liquid.

I went to the soaking room and was filled with the presence of the Lord. Jesus poured out silvery dust all over my body. I went to the dance floor to dance with Father. I was wearing silvery royal clothes. I went to the throne room to see the four faces of God. Smoke was all around and a huge wing of one of the cherubim's covered me. I cast my crown before Father.

218

I traveled back in time with Jesus to Mount Sinai where Moses and the Israelites were camping in hundreds of tents.

Jesus asked me, "Do you know why my people died in the wilderness?"

I said, "Because they murmured, grumbled and complained."

Jesus replied, "Yes, but also because they did not trust my Father that He can do all this for them to take them out and bring them to the Promised Land. Don't be like them; believe with all of your heart."

"Yes Lord", I said.

AMEN!

We went inside one tent where a woman had a bad fever. When Jesus put a compress on her forehead, the fever left and the woman was healed.

Corona Virus in Italy

Jesus and I continued our journey to Italy, where a woman in the hospital had many tubes on her. She had the corona virus. When Jesus gave her a drink from a light green vial she vomited.

Jesus asked her, "Do you believe Who I AM?"

She said, "Who are You?"

Jesus, "I AM the way to life. Open your heart and receive Me."

Woman, "Lord, I've done so many horrible things in my life."
Jesus said: "There is nothing that you've done that I can't forgive."

Woman, "Forgive me Lord."

The woman got up from the bed and kneeled down before Jesus and gave her heart to Him. Praise God.

Jesus touched her head and said, "You are forgiven my child."

Entering Jerusalem

I went into my garden to a beautiful green field with flowers and mountains. Jesus put a beryl necklace around my neck. We danced and twirled around and around and around.

We went to Jerusalem and walked on a road until we got to a white brick house. There was a woman laying on a bed sick with a very high fever.

I asked Jesus what is her sickness and the Lord replied, "Diphtheria. A witch cursed this house."

Warrior angels picked up several snakes and put them in bags taking them away. I took out from my pouch a florescent green vial and gave her to drink while Jesus touched her forehead. We waited for a while until the woman stood up completely healed. She marveled at this miracle and knelt down in front of Jesus. Jesus blessed her and I gave her a scroll.

We continued our journey through Jerusalem arriving at a fountain where we drank some water and rested for a while. A few feet from us was a boy crying that had a wound on his right arm. He was crying and screaming of pain.Jesus and I approached the boy and He touched his arm. Seconds later the wound disappeared and the boy stopped crying. He ran quickly towards his mother.

Two angels appeared with scrolls that wanted us to follow them. Jesus and I mounted our horses and we journeyed to an open field where several angels placed a huge net on the ground. It looked like they wanted to trap some kind of beast. A dragon appeared; hit the net and the angels pulled the ropes, trapping it.

Another tall angel was holding the net on a pole. Jesus signaled him to lower the pole. He opened the pole and the dragon was very frightened. Jesus took his sword and cut open the beast's belly. He took out a twenty by thirty-foot, bright, white diamond. We took this diamond to my heart garden. Jesus told me to chop open the diamond revealing a scroll in the middle. We took the scroll out and rolled it out like a carpet. It was a sparkling diamond scroll. I looked closely to read the scroll and I saw a drawing of the prayer mountain.

Praise God for He is worthy of all glory.

The Fiery Scroll in the Heart Garden

I went in the spirit to my heart garden, to see sawgrass scattered around.

(True facts about Sawgrass: it's a tall, slender plant that can reach up to ten feet high. It grows quickly and densely in water. Sawgrass is famous for its sharp points that run along the edges of its leaves. These teeth can cut you upon contact – therefore the name sawgrass.)

I saw hundreds of hunter angels pulling them from the roots, throwing them over the wall out of my garden and burning them. Dozens and dozens were uprooted and burned. This process took a while, as they were so many sawgrass plants everywhere.

221

Next, I saw Jesus taking flare scrolls and dropping them in the empty holes all over the garden. The fire from the scrolls was burning all the sawgrass seeds.

I walked with Jesus through the river collecting buckets of rocks of gold, emeralds, amethyst, rubies and white diamonds. We dropped them in all the holes. Then healing angels came with big pitchers and filled the holes with anointed oil. Trees started to grow out of the ground: gold trees, amethyst trees, emerald trees, ruby trees and white diamond trees.

Gold represents purity and richness.

Amethyst represents purification and perfection.

Emerald represents vitality and the life of God, patience and unconditional love.

Rubies represent vitality and wellness.

There were three buckets full of precious stones and gold and silver that we exchanged on the sea of glass. We exchanged them for new oil that I put in my emerald green jar, a hunting spear, six scrolls and a book of paints and brushes. I went to wisdom heights and asked what the book was.

She said, "More revelation and knowledge and hidden secrets and mysteries of the Kingdom of God."

I asked Jesus about the six scrolls.

He said, "Take three scrolls and plant them in the garden and the other three eat them.

So, I took three scrolls and planted them by the tree where I always meet with Jesus and ate the rest of them.

I looked at the new spear weapon I received and said, "I wonder what this could do?"

I mounted my other battle fiery horse Eshe Ruah and flew over a valley. Inside the valley was a python-beast slithering around. I shoved the spear in its eye. The python became petrified and fell into dust.

Meeting the Twenty-four Kings and My Scroll of Destiny

I walked with Jesus through a river where He picked up a huge fish. We sat on a white sheet, fried it and ate it. After that we went down the rapids, until we went over a waterfall and into a pond. We played in the water splashing around for a while and then I followed Jesus behind the waterfall into a cave. Jesus was illuminating the path with a torch. We arrived at a door where He gave me a golden key, opening the door to a room full of silvery scrolls. Together with the angels we collected the scrolls and brought them to the record room to be recorded and signed.

Jesus and AI took them to the Court of Kings. There were many Kings sitting in their regal chairs. I distributed twenty-four scrolls to them.

I took one of the scrolls to Father's chambers pinned it up on the fireplace and it rolled all the way into the middle of the floor. I asked the Father what was written on it.

He said, "Everything you've ever done and do in the past, present and future with AI, your destiny scroll, storms that you encounter, rising above the storms, defeating the enemy, strategies for war, battles, angelic encounters, miracles, prayer mountain, timeline, treasures, prosperity.

Each scroll that you gave to these kings are specific assignments in Heaven to be brought on earth for different times and seasons."

I saw angels come holding pitchers and pouring oils over the scrolls.

After that they all pointed the scrolls at me (I was wearing golden royal clothes with my golden crown on my head) and electricity and waves of Heaven's frequency came out of them and started to flow from the bottom of my feet all the way up.

The kings said to me, "Be filled with the frequency of Heaven, remain in this frequency, fasting is important, remain single-minded and defeat the enemy in the battlefield of the mind."

Healing in Galilee and meeting the Cloud of Witnesses

I saw Yeshua, my love, by Galilee Lake. He was drinking water with His hands; He gave me some to drink also. After that He walked on a pier, gazing at the lake like He was waiting for something when a boat approached the shore. We both got into the boat and I saw Peter, Thomas and Nathaniel from Cana in Galilee. They all threw a net on the right side of the boat and caught multitudes of fish. They loaded the boat with fish and we all began to sort them and put them in buckets.

When we finished, the boat docked and we put the fish in a big cart. The cart was pulled by donkeys, taking us to a market where we sold the fish and mingled with the crowd. We saw many people buying and selling fruit and vegetables. Some men came in the middle of the market carrying a man on a stretcher and put him down in front of us. The man had a missing left leg.

I looked at Jesus and He smiled at me. Instinctively I knew He wanted me to do a miracle.

I looked at the man and asked, "How long have you been without a leg?"

The man said, "Twelve years."

I said, "Wait no more, this is your day for a miracle."

Out of the crowd came an angel with a leg. I took the leg attached it to the man's hip and he was made whole. The man stood up shocked and jumped for joy. Praise God for this miracle! He hugged Jesus with tears in his eyes.

I went to the Father's chambers by the fireplace. Al was here. It was a magnificent awe of the presence of God. Angels brought us lemon tea and cookies. The door opened and a cloud of witnesses walked in: Bob Jones with his angels, Kathryn Kuhlman, Smith Wigglesworth, Isaiah and Elijah. Wow Praise God for them!

Father declared, "The cloud of witnesses prays for you, intercedes for you, day and night, they sustain you."

Bob Jones said to me, "Precious daughter of God, the book is coming along well, you shall know more; the Seven Spirits of God are there to assist you."

Kathleen Kuhlman said to me, "Beautiful daughter of Jesus, take this oil (she put all over my hands and head). You shall heal many people."

Smith Wigglesworth, Isaiah and Elijah gave Al a scroll.

Father spoke to us, "My precious ones, you are on the right track, don't worry about anything, you shall make progress, I shall provide for both of you supernaturally all the finances you need for the prayer mountain and other projects I have for you.

The cloud of witnesses intercedes for you day and night. Be encouraged. Love one another as I love you. Don't let the devil steal from you anymore. Recognize his evil schemes. Don't let the sun go down on your anger. Come to me daily and drink from Me. Be filled with My

breath. Don't let the spirit of criticism come between you. Love each other as I love you with pure love. Be blessed my children."

To God the Father, Jesus Christ and the Holy Spirit be the Glory, honor and power. Amen!

On the Mountain of God the Father where He sheds His glory

Yeshua was under my tree in the garden waiting for me. We walked along a pathway until we reached a waterfall, where we both became white eagles and flew around doing accolades and acrobatics in the air, having fun. We reached the other side of the waterfall and became us again.

Jesus said, "Follow Me."

We arrived at a bridge across from a mountain. On the bridge I saw multitudes of angels coming with Elijah, Moses and Enoch. The angels carried what looked like a huge mirror on their shoulders and when they leaned it on the mountain it became a door. We all walked through the door; Enoch was illuminating the path for us with a torch. We arrived at a platform on another mountain and climbed it until we reached the top. Here the glory of God was indescribable; gold all around and multicolors that I had not seen before. I bowed down before the Lord, cast my crown and was hugging and kissing Father's feet.

After that, Father and Jesus took me to the bridal chambers where I asked to be purified. I received a mantle of fire from the Father. Father placed a crown of fire on my head and put a scepter of fire in my hand.

He said, "Come and rule with me."

I said, "Who Am I to do this Father?"

He said, "Come and sit with me, don't be afraid."

So, I sat next to the Father on my royal seat. Al was there also.

Father said, "You shall judge saints and angels."

I was in new Heavenly garments with my scepter and there was a line-up of saints and angels coming forward.

Swimming in the Big Waterfall Again

Today I dived into the big waterfall in my garden with my Lord Yeshua. He went to the bottom and picked up a huge trunk. Six other angels came to help us. We put the trunk on a rock at the edge of the waterfall. Yeshua opened the trunk and took out the following:

- A dagger of gold with a purple handle
- A scroll that said: Identity
- A huge purple diamond

He told me to eat the scroll, which tasted bittersweet. He took me to the throne room of the Father Who was sitting glorious on the throne, that had a blazing light emanating from it. Seraphim and Cherubim were there. We exchanged the purple diamond for a purple scroll.

We went to the record room to have it recorded. The purple scroll is a specific mandate that will be revealed in time.

Beryl Stones

I went to my garden where Jesus was drinking water with His hands while He was looking for something.

I said, "Lord what are you looking for?"

He just smiled at me and splashed me with water and we played in the river.

After that He said, "Follow Me!"

He picked up beryl objects from the river. Angels were stirring up the river making the whole river a fluorescent, beryl color.

A small boat came by and Jesus said, "Hop in"

We went down the rapids so fast but then we shifted to where both of us were flying around this valley above a city in Israel by the Mediterranean Sea. We walked through narrow streets in Haifa, arriving at a house with a white gate. Jesus and I entered a house where a woman had stomach cancer. I gave the woman to drink from the beryl object and she threw up the cancer, becoming perfectly healed. She fell down at Jesus feet giving Him all the praise.

Jesus and I continued our journey in the downtown market of this city. A man was convulsing and was full of evil spirits. My warrior angels Erelim were here with their swords out. Weird animals and creatures came out of this man that we all chopped with our swords. The man came to sit next to Jesus on a bench. Jesus touched his head and blessed him and we went on our way to more journeys in the spirit.

Blessed be the Lord Jesus Christ the Son of God and God the Father Amen!

Oak Trees, Diamonds and More Treasures

I went to the dance floor where Jesus danced with me. I was wearing a light golden and white dress with a white crown.

I said, "Lord, I want to feel your love, teach me and make me feel Your multidimensional love, expand Your love in my heart."

He said, "Come."

We danced in twirls until Father came and danced with me until we all blended together in the love of them and united like a funnel of multicolors; the color of the rainbow. The seven Spirits of God were present there. Angels were playing instruments. All the memories, all the hurts and all the fragments were taken out of me and healed by Jesus love. He then put me on a table and put His hand on my chest and Jesus' hand was vibrating inside of me with His love. Father's hand was touching my heart also. I could see fragments coming out of me and being healed one by one.

I went to my heart garden where there was a big hole in the ground. Out of this hole came out shadows of insecurity, anxiety, hurt, disappointments and fragments from the past. My warrior angels were there also. A portal was opened and those dark shadows were taken into another dimension.

Jesus then took four fiery scrolls and placed them at the bottom of each corner of the hole. Sparks of fire came out of the scrolls and burned all the seeds associated with the dark shadows.

As this process continued, the hole was getting smaller and smaller. Angels were pouring oil with the fragrance of honey into the hole. And finally, the hole was closed.

Yeshua and I then went swimming in the waterfall. An oak tree was planted in this place in my heart garden.

Oak trees symbolize strength, morale, endurance, eternity, honor, liberty, hospitality, faith, and virtue – The oak is the king of trees.

I went back to my heart garden where Jesus took out a box, opened it to show me a letter from God the Father that said, "My dear one, My precious one, your healing is here, step into it, stop struggling with it. Rest in Me, go on a fast for three days with water. Stop watching TV, internet, the tablet and just rest in Me. I love you with an infinite unending love."

I then walked with Jesus by a river where we sat under a tree and hugged.He told me to rest. As I rested, I watched the river flowing down with a shooting sound of water. I caressed a deer that approached us, and gave her something to eat. We skipped stones.Jesus told me to watch, as a fish came and dropped a bead in my hand that Jesus put on my necklace.

Jesus got up and said, "Follow Me."

We crossed the river, but this time we walked on the water. We went up a small hill pushing the branches out of the way arriving at a steep valley. As I looked in the distance, clouds moved and a huge metal foot landed where we were.

I asked, "Lord what is this?"

He replied, "Watch."

It was a five-hundred-mile tall angel wearing full body armor. I wanted to see his face up close, so Jesus, knowing my thoughts, took me up to look at the angel's face. He was holding a shiny, silvery sword with an amber handle. We followed the angel as he walked in the valley. When he took steps his foot mark was as big as a half mile. He stopped at a beach where in the distance was an unusual dragon. The angel wrestled with it and dragged it into the ocean. He ended up choking it. The angel brought its body onto a beach. I took my sword out and cut open its belly. A six-foot ruby came out rolling down to where Jesus was standing. Other angels came, picked up the ruby and carried it to my finance mountain.

Jesus smashed the ruby into thousands of pieces and put them on a conveyer belt. On the other end of the conveyer belt was another angel that was sorting through the rubies. Buckets full of rubies were taken to a room where there were robes of saints displayed. Angels took the rubies and made ten robes for saints. I tried one on and it was magnificent. The sleeves were with silver and gold and the entire robe was shiny with different shades of red.

What an awesome Father and Jesus. Blessed be His name!

Jesus and I were white eagles again flying around in accolades, dancing in the air. We took a fast dive into the waterfall and under water we became us. We came out of the water and flew as white eagles again. We dived again in the water and we became us again. We repeated this process one more time, and then I followed Jesus swimming under water. He came out of the water inside of a cave and He stretched out His hand to help me out. Jesus was holding a torch in His hand and was illuminating this pathway inside of the cave. I met Elijah and he gave me a scroll. I put it in my pouch. We walked further to arrive at a wall where Jesus opened a small door. He took a silver box out, opened it, revealing a red medallion with a gold stamp in the middle.

On the stamp was written, "My warrior one, My precious one, sealed with the blood of Jesus."

WOW Praise God!

He put the medallion on my neck, took a bottle from His pocket and put a few drops on my hands and feet. I love my Lord so much.

Waterfall Ecstasy

I went swimming with Jesus again in the waterfall. The scenic waterfall was five-hundred-feet wide that gushed over rocks, surging and plunging down the mountain. It had a beautiful serenity-pool at the bottom that was white because it was mixed with air.

We both went into a cave where Jesus poured a red-green liquid over my body, took a large diamond and put it in my chest and gave me His blood to drink. My whole body was transformed.
Then He gave me three green scrolls. I ate one of them and took the rest to the record room to be recorded.

I went back to the waterfall where Jesus and I went behind it. I could see the water crashing down in front of me. I put my hand under the water and white small diamonds formed into my hand.

Jesus jumped on the rock behind the falls and prompted me to follow Him. Yeshua was holding a torch in His hand and I was behind Him. We went down spiral stairs deep into the cave. Angels were here with many scrolls. Jesus took the scrolls and stuck them into my heart delivering me from a dark cloud that was over my head. I received a healing scroll that was dripping oil and I ate it.

Walking with Father and Jesus in the Garden of Eden

I went walking with Jesus and Father in the Garden of Eden. Al was there also. An elephant came by and brought me a fruit to eat. It was yellow and red and tasted like honeydew. We walked further where a lion approached us. He was holding a white scroll in his mouth tied with a red ribbon. Father took the scroll and we all got transported to His mountain.

The best I could describe it, it was full of the Glory of God beyond the seven colors of the rainbow: yellow, blue, red, orange, green, indigo and violet. The mountain was the color of jasper and the predominant color was gold. The glory of God was so thick and full of golden light.

A Seraphim angel took the scroll and threw it into the glory. Thunder and lightning changed the entire atmosphere of the mountain and my body became full of gold dust from top to bottom. Everyone around me was full of gold dust. Then, Father, Jesus and I were flying like white eagles to arrive at the throne room. Father walked up and sat on His seat of authority. I fell to my face on the sapphire floor. Father nudged me to come up to sit next to Him.

Jesus came and said, "Let's distribute these ruby robes to the saints."

An angel brought the robes and we gave them to all of the saints that gathered before the throne. Jesus also gave crowns and scepters to the saints.

Praise God the Father and Jesus Christ the Holy One!

Another Journey to India

I was caught up to the Heavens and looked down at a map of the world. I asked Jesus where we shall go today who needs help. In an instant, Jesus took me to India. We walked through all the busy streets and markets where lots of people were caring for their carts, selling goods. Not far from us, an old man was groaning with pain. A vegetable cart had fallen on his right hip wounding him.

A warrior angel picked up the cart and freed him. Another angel took the man to the side of a curb. I took oil from my emerald green jar and poured it over his hip. The wound closed and the pain was gone. The man was astonished and asked me in his language how is this possible. In the supernatural realm there is no barrier to foreign languages.

I said, "Jesus is the one who gave you life and healed you. Do you know Who He is?"

The man replied, "No."

"He is the only true God, He is the Way, the Truth and the Life who died on the cross for you and shed His blood so that your sins might be forgiven. Would you like to receive Him as your Lord and Savior?"

The man agreed.

An angel brought a sanctified robe and Jesus put it on his shoulders. He also gave him a crown and a scepter.

Jesus said to the man, "Welcome in my Father's Kingdom."

Traveling with Jesus to Mauritania

I began walking on a wide road through a forest, ending up at a lake where there was an ancient-looking boat. Yeshua, some angels and I got into the boat and traveled over the North Atlantic Ocean, ending up in Mauritania. We walked up on a beach, arriving at a battle sight. Two tribes were fighting and killing one another when time froze and the tribal people froze. I saw an arrow suspended in the air. I looked to the right and a man was lying dead by a tree with an axe stuck in his head. I took the axe out, which actually made a noise when I took it out. I poured oil from the emerald green jar that I have on my side and his wound gradually healed and closed. I laid my hand on his chest and raised him from the dead.

I turned to see another man dead with an arrow stuck in his neck. I took the arrow out. Yeshua poured a liquid over his wound and he was healed. I raised him from the dead the same way like the other man. Time unfroze and all of the people looked at us astonished, unable to speak.

Jesus walked by the eight men, putting His hand on their heads and they all fell.

After a while they all got up and one man took us to meet their chief. I preached the gospel to them and they all became children of God, followers of Yeshua. Jesus gave them crowns, scepters and new robes. Angels sanctified their land by pouring a shimmery liquid over the entire place. The Seven Spirits of God came to tutor the tribe.

PRAISE GOD FOR ANOTHER VICTORY IN JESUS NAME!

Traveling to Africa

A boat came and Jesus told me to hop in. We traveled through a river and marsh and after a while we arrived in Africa. We got out of the boat and walked on a desert road, arriving at a place where a group of army soldiers were ready to shoot thirty Christians. Angels came quickly and dropped the machine guns out of their hands.

We transported the whole group to a safe place in a forest. We were all sitting by a fireplace when Jesus gave the leader of the group a scroll. Out of the bush came a guide and took them to a safe place. Praise God for this rescue.

I was in my heart garden walking thought the river with Yeshua and Father.

As I looked around there was a small cave in the ground. Jesus and I looked down to see a crocodile hidden there. An angel came with a pole with a rope attached to it, grabbed the beast by the neck and took it to another dimension. There were also several white snakes and other snakes that angels took away in bags. I walked further into the cave and saw a monster. My warrior angel took it out in chains.

Yeshua put his blood all over and cleaned it. The cave closed up to become a hill. A tall silver tree rose up where the cave had been.

"You are a hiding place for me; You, Lord, preserve me from trouble, You surround me with songs and shouts of deliverance. Selah [pause, and calmly think of that]!

I [the Lord] will instruct you and teach you in the way you should go; I will counsel you with My eye upon you.

Be not like the horse or the mule, which lack understanding, which must have their mouths held firm with bit and bridle, or else they will not come with you.

Many are the sorrows of the wicked, but he who trusts in, relies on, and confidently leans on the Lord shall be compassed about with mercy and with loving-kindness. Psalm 32: 7-10

Defeating a beast in the clouds

Today all the warrior angels that I work with, including Sons of God, Michael and Malachim Uriel angel went to battle a huge beast in the clouds. I couldn't see the beast that clearly as it hid behind some clouds, only once in a while popping its head out to growl at us. The beast was surrounded by millions of angels. We were waiting for Yeshua and Father's strategy on how to take out this beast.

Yeshua walked up to us with a white scroll in His hand and gave it to Michael the Archangel. Michael took the scroll and passed it to all of us. The scroll multiplied into millions so each of us could read it.

The scroll described steps on how to destroy this beast.

Michael made the first move taking his fiery-lighting sword and impaled the beast's head with it. The rest of us followed him like a tidal wave attacking it.

Many other beasts appeared. I chopped many snake's heads as I was riding Eshe Ruah, my fiery horse. A net took the remaining beasts away.

237

The dark atmosphere was lifted and the sun came out. I looked on the ground where there were diamonds like icicles. Angels gathered them in big sacks. I asked Jesus where He wanted me to take them and He told me to take them to the sea of glass. When I did, I received a trunk full of treasures. I also took some of the diamonds to the treasure room in Heaven. I took the trunk of treasures to the Father's chambers.

Father, Jesus, Al and I opened the trunk where Al took out a new sword. When he moved it around, it made a noise like a tornado and things were spinning around at the same time.

I took out a golden sword. I had my gauntlet metal glove on and when I was holding this sword my whole body became gold. This gold on my body gave me a double shield of protection against the enemy. I also took out a medallion and a treasure box with gold coins. I asked Yeshua what He wanted me to do with the coins and He told me to take them to my heart garden and plant them in the ground were the roots had been that I pulled out yesterday. When I did that, gold trees grew up in the garden.

Praise God for victory in the name of out Yeshua Hamashiach!

The Orb

I journeyed in the spirit on a boat with Jesus and angels. I started in the river that's in my heart garden. After we traveled in the boat, we walked on a wide road with multitudes of warrior angels. We arrived on a beach where far in the ocean I could see a beast; strange looking one like a big whale but with wings.I saw an angel shooting a harpoon, pinning the beast into its place. Then Michael the archangel cut the beast in two, revealing an orb that angels brought to the beach.

This orb which was ten-feet wide and long of a light-golden fluorescent color. Yeshua said that I should take this orb with me at all times to create portals of Heaven everywhere I go.

I put it on all my mountains:

personal, family, financial, art, entertainment and our ministry mountain. I also took the orb to our prayer mountain.

Everywhere the orb was, a portal formed and multitudes of angels came.

Another Ecstasy in Jerusalem

I went to the bridal chamber where I was purified with fire by a Seraphim angel. I went on the dance floor where Father, Jesus and I were spinning in a funnel until we all became one.

I went to my heart garden where Jesus and I walked through the river. Father came and they poured water over my head purifying me. After a while we got into a boat and went down the rapids, stopped at the river bank and walked through a forest. Messenger angels accompanied us bringing scrolls.

We got to an open field where there was a white chariot with white horses waiting for us. The ride was very fast through time and space. We went through a portal above Israel. Hundreds of white scrolls begin to unfold from Heaven rolling all the way down to the streets of Jerusalem. The scrolls multiplied as they came down and were placed in different parts of the city. More portals opened from above pouring pitchers of oil out over Israel.

All the scrolls were being pinned down to the ground as hundreds of white horses came and filled the entire city.

The Palace Ecstasy

I saw wheels within wheels spinning around with eyes on it. I saw the sapphire pavement and the feet of Father. I saw myself sitting at His right hand on my throne. My eyes were full of light that became fire.

Jesus came with a horse-carriage to take me for a ride. There were four white horses and the carriage was like from the 1800's with two seats, black on the outside. We rode for a while. I was wearing my golden garments and a golden crown. Jesus was dressed in what looked like Victorian-era clothes.

We arrived at a palace welcomed by angels. Inside there were gothic, gold trimmed walls about fifty yards tall. Pink and blue angels were flying around. We went up a set of wide stairs that had angels lined up on the edge of the stairs. We arrived inside a ballroom where kings and queens were dancing a waltz. Father was there also dancing with us. The Seven Spirits of God enveloped us and were moving around in waves in-between us. The cloud of witnesses was present. Angels formed a funnel and I was inside this funnel twirling around.

I went to the Father's chambers enjoying His presence. Apostle Paul walked in to give me a scroll. When I unrolled it, Father held one end of it as I was holding the other end. I found myself inside the prayer mountain overlooking a lake.

Spiritual Warfare above Israel, Jordan and Egypt

I went to my favorite place in the spirit to the big waterfall where Jesus was waiting for me on the bridge. He poured oil over my head and pointed out something in the distance that looked like a hydra. Warrior angels on horses and chariots appeared all around us. Jesus and I got on a chariot and went to where this principality was above Israel, Jordan and Egypt that was keeping people blind to the Gospel and to the truth of Whom Jesus Christ really is.

This beast was taunting us as the warrior angels surrounded it while we waited for the strategy of battle.

A warrior angel brought the scroll that multiplied so each of us could read the plan.

The battle began with a light from above pinning it down, allowing warrior angels to chop its heads. I chopped three heads off. A spear appeared in my hand that I threw into one hydra's eye. The beast ended up exploding into thousands of pieces. The remains were gathered by angels that took them to a different dimension.

A five-hundred-mile tall angel came to replace this principality.

Traveling with Jesus to New York

We landed in downtown New York more precisely in Times Square. We walked around the busy streets full of lights and commercialized advertisements, cars, busses, bikers, etc.

I looked up at a skyscraper and I was thinking, are we going to go inside one of these buildings? Jesus nudged me to follow Him down the street.

We entered this old building on the first floor into a room where a woman was bedridden with seven diseases. She was sick with lung cancer, lyme disease, arthritis, glaucoma (eye disease), liver disease, blood disease and heart arrhythmia. Jesus instructed me to speak life over her body and release the frequency of Heaven into her body. I hesitated so He told me to hold my hand up and He imparted vibration and frequency into my hand. I held my hand over the woman and all the vibrations entered her body. All seven evil spirits (seven diseases) came out one at the time and my warrior angels chained them and took them to spiritual prisons to another dimension in the supernatural realm.

I saw Jesus operating on this woman and taking the lung tumor out, then sewing her flesh back. I poured oil from my jar over her body and waited.

She got up, not looking pale and rugged anymore with disease. Her whole countenance changed. She went to another room, ecstatic with joy, where her family was mingling around talking and being worried about her.

She said, "I am completely healed, look at me I am healed."

Everyone looked at her like she was nuts.

Then I made myself visible and said, "Jesus is the one who healed you. Would you like to receive Him as your Lord and Savior?"

She hesitated. After that I took her to the cross and showed her the blood of Jesus and I mentioned that He paid the price and took all of her diseases on the cross for her.

When she looked at Jesus, she fell at His feet and said, "Yes, I receive Him, You are the Lord, Jesus Christ, the Son of God!"

We got transported back to her apartment and I led her into prayer of salvation.

Jesus appeared to her and put a robe of righteousness over her shoulders and a crown over her head and said, "Welcome to My Father's Kingdom my child."

Rescuing women from human trafficking

I went in the spirit to the suspension bridge by the outstanding waterfall. The mist from it was enveloping us. There is a power and brilliance in the tranquility, a place of stillness even in the roar of the water.

I crossed the bridge to the other side to a cave. On the right side was a platform where warrior angles gathered. Angels on horses lined up in rows of three. A chariot of fire came and picked us up. We traveled over many clouds, mountains and hills until we arrived in Thailand. We were on a mission to rescue twenty women from human trafficking. We walked on the poor streets of Nong Khai in Northeast Thailand. The frequency from Heaven that we brought started to spread everywhere and many women came out of huts and followed us. As we walked further, we saw a man ready to strike a woman but an angel froze his body so he couldn't move. We transported all the women to a meadow in a valley and took them to a safe house.

I told them, "You have a chance for a better life. Jesus is here and He died on the cross for you to set you free. His blood cleanses you, makes you pure, follow Him."

Jesus took a golden bottle and poured a liquid over all their heads and their bodies transforming them in a Heavenly frequency. They knelt down at His feet, repenting and gave their hearts to Him. They all received new garments, robes, scepters and crowns.

Traveling to Ashdod in Israel

After Jesus and I swam and splashed by the waterfall we got out and sat on the beach. An angel came with a small, ornate, wooden box. Jesus took out a map of Israel and a golden bottle with a long neck.

As we looked at the map Jesus pointed to a city between Tel Aviv and Ashkelon. He rolled up the map and we translated to Ashdod a city on the coast of Mediterranean Sea. As we walked on this street, we entered a house to find a woman with cancer. Her family was outside the room worried for her.

Jesus said to her in her spirit, "I Am. Do you believe I can heal you?"

Her spirit said, "Who are you, Lord?"

"I Am Yeshua, who took away your sicknesses. Your ancestors rejected me, but don't do the same mistake." He showed her in a vision how His blood poured out on the cross for her to be set free.

The woman said, "I believe."

Jesus took the bottle and gave it to her to drink. The frequency from the liquid came all over her body and she started to vibrate until stillness came upon her. When she opened her eyes, she was completely healed.

She came out of her room shouting, "I am healed, Jesus healed me!"Her family saw that she was fine.

Praise God for another miracle.

Journey to Israel Again

I went to my heart garden where Jesus was already waiting for me under this magnificent tree on a white sheet. We were having a great picnic. Yeshua gave me strawberries to eat. Father came and joined us also. The Seven Spirits of God together with Wisdom and her Handmaidens came to fellowship with us.

After the picnic, Yeshua unrolled a map showing us where we are supposed to go next. He rolled up the map, gave it to Al and he put it underneath his armor. Al mounted his white battle horse Whitey and left with his warrior angels.

Wisdom gave me a honey-like substance to drink from a pitcher. She said that this drink is to strengthen me. We all mounted our horses and went to battle. We arrived by the Mediterranean Sea in an open field. Yeshua unrolled the map together with other angels. The map was thirty-feet long by thirty-feet wide. When the map was unrolled, a light from Heaven illuminated it. The light became a multicolored rainbow and started to vibrate with the frequency of Heaven.

Out of a portal came down Enoch, Jeremiah and Isaiah. The Sons of God, Banai-Elohim angels, came also together with the Archangel

Michael. We all gazed at the sea as a beast with multiple heads came out of the water taunting us. Multiple chariots of angels together with Sons of God and Michael surrounded this beast and threw spears at it. Thousands of spears and arrows were stuck into its body. Al flew with Whitey and with one strike chopped off the main head of the hydra.The rest of the heads formed a circle and came at us. I threw my sword up in the air and it spun like a helicopter propeller chopping off all the heads.

Next there were two dragons flying around. I killed them both with my golden sword. One of them I took to the beach, cut open its belly that revealed diamonds with multicolors. Angels put the diamonds in sacks and took them to the Way of the Eagle Mountain.

I asked Father what we are going to do with all these diamonds.

Father said, "Millions of dollars will come for us to do all we need to do at Way of the Eagle ministries. Prophesy your future according to what I have promised. Create wealth with your mouth."

CONCLUSION

As you engage with the frequency of light your whole being gets transformed. Soak in the spirit and come to Heaven to meet Father, Jesus, the Holy Spirit and angels face to face.

You are a spirit being. Imagine yourself as you step out of your natural body and engage with your spiritual body, as you are a being of light just like your Heavenly Father is.

Develop your spiritual senses, hearing, seeing, touch, smell and taste.

Don't let religionists, scoffers, nay-sayers or fools keep you from experiencing the greatest experiences in life that you can imagine.

The world, religion, people, things, can't offer anyone joy or life or eternity. Chart your destiny with God onto your own Journey with Him.

"But you are a chosen race, a royal priesthood, a dedicated nation, [God's] own purchased, special people, that you may set forth the wonderful deeds and display the virtues and perfections of Him Who called you out of darkness into His marvelous light." 1 Peter 2:9

"But I say, walk and live [habitually] in the [Holy] Spirit [responsive to and controlled and guided by the Spirit]; then you will certainly not gratify the cravings and desires of the flesh (of human nature without God)." Galatians 5:16

He's ready to go when you are.

"Do two walk together except they make an appointment and have agreed?" Amos 3:3

Hope to see you out there. Let's shine like Jesus!

REFERENCES

Ian Clayton – Son of Thunder Ministry

Kanaan Ministries – South Africa

More Books to help in your Journey with God

THE WAY

"I have many wonders in store for you. You will see when you come to Me. I do not withhold. I am here. I will not abandon you. I long to be with you. Come, and I will show you your path; your destiny. You will know why you are here. I will tell you. Come expecting gifts. I have so many things to tell you; to reveal to you; to give you. Come."

… GOD – from Chapter 7

"My rare ones, do not think that you are not of much importance. I call out to the hearts of every person to come to Me. Rest with Me. Allow Me to calm the storms that come against you. Allow Me to clear the paths and quench your thirst. What you search for is here. It rests with Me and in this Kingdom. The world cannot touch your heart but with a dead finger. My hand contains life everlasting. Reach out for it, and it is there. I will not refuse you nor reject you. I will soothe your wounds. Come into Heaven and accept your inheritance. It waits for you. Your crowns are here. Your treasures are here. Do not abandon them, as your portion is set before you for a reason. Your inheritance is offered to you now, to partake of as you walk in the world.

"If you will come to Me, the treasures of Heaven belong to you. Walk in your gardens and mountains. Eat of the fruits that are ripe. So much waits for you. Come."

... GOD – from Chapter 10

———————————◆◆◆◆———————————

"The Way was virtually lost into history, saved for a few who learned how to walk with God, in His image.

God will speak to you directly on how you can find this lost ancient Way!

He'll show you The Way to come and visit with Him face-to-face in His throne room!

He'll teach you how to walk into Heaven whenever you like, to partake of all of its treasures!

You'll learn how to see and have angels protect you and work with you!

God will teach you how to tap into unlimited wealth that He's had waiting for you before you were born!

God will show you how only He can provide you with the secrets to life and success, as He says that the ways and secrets that man provides are a fool's errand and have become their powerless gods.

Follow The Way now and step into immortality!" from the Introduction

This book provides keys and messages from God on how anyone can develop their spiritual senses and capabilities, with a final goal to walk with Him face-to-face which is His desire for everyone.

THE SILVER BULLET OF GOD

BOOK IN CHRISTIAN UNIVERSITIES, COLLEGES AND CHURCH GROUPS AROUND THE WORLD IN OVER 190 COUNTRIES

- How to operate in the Supernatural
- How to develop your Spiritual Gifts
- Holy Spirit Baptism
- How to work with the Holy Spirit
- How to Heal the Sick
- How to Cast out and imprison Evil Spirits
- How to Free People from Spiritual Prisons…
    - including Yourself
- How to Raise the Dead
- How to do High Level,
    - Ground Level
        - and Occult Level Spiritual Warfare
- How to recognize and deal with the Wolf
- What a real Christian and Church should be doing…
    - according to God
- Equip yourself for the Five-Fold Ministry…
    - postle, Prophet, Evangelist, Pastor, Teacher
- Visit the Heavens now
- Prayer and Fasting to Change Your City and Nation

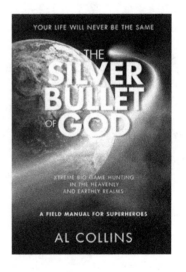

- Spiritual Mapping
- How to Work with Angels
- Who has Salvation or Damnation... according to God's Word
- How to Recover what the Enemy has Stolen
- Learn the Most successful Evangelism process... SAFARI
- How to Develop Your Relationship with God
- How to Fulfill Your Destiny with God

THE GOD FARM

GREAT ADVENTURE NOVEL FOR ALL AGES

Two kids discover reality in the most unlikely place where they're taught how to become gods.

Setting out on adventures in different dimensions, these two new gods defeat wizards, monsters and other nasties afflicting Earth to rescue those trapped in their fantasy worlds of superstition and illusion, setting them free to become gods themselves.

Will a final epic war destroy them and the planet before they can stop it and move onto more important things... like living for eternity in peace, governing their own personal universes?

Take a detour onto the road to The God Farm.

They're waiting there to teach you how to become a god yourself.

If you like J.R.R. Tolkien's The Lord of the Rings, C.S. Lewis' Narnia and William Young's The Shack, then you won't be able to put down the riveting adventures of these heroic God Operators.

For more information go to:

www.wayoftheeagle.org

CPSIA information can be obtained
at www.ICGtesting.com
Printed in the USA
LVHW040418051020
667928LV00018B/763